RAREST

of

DIAMONDS

GARY CARUSO

with a foreword by Jimmy Carter

LONGSTREET PRESS, INC.
Atlanta, Georgia

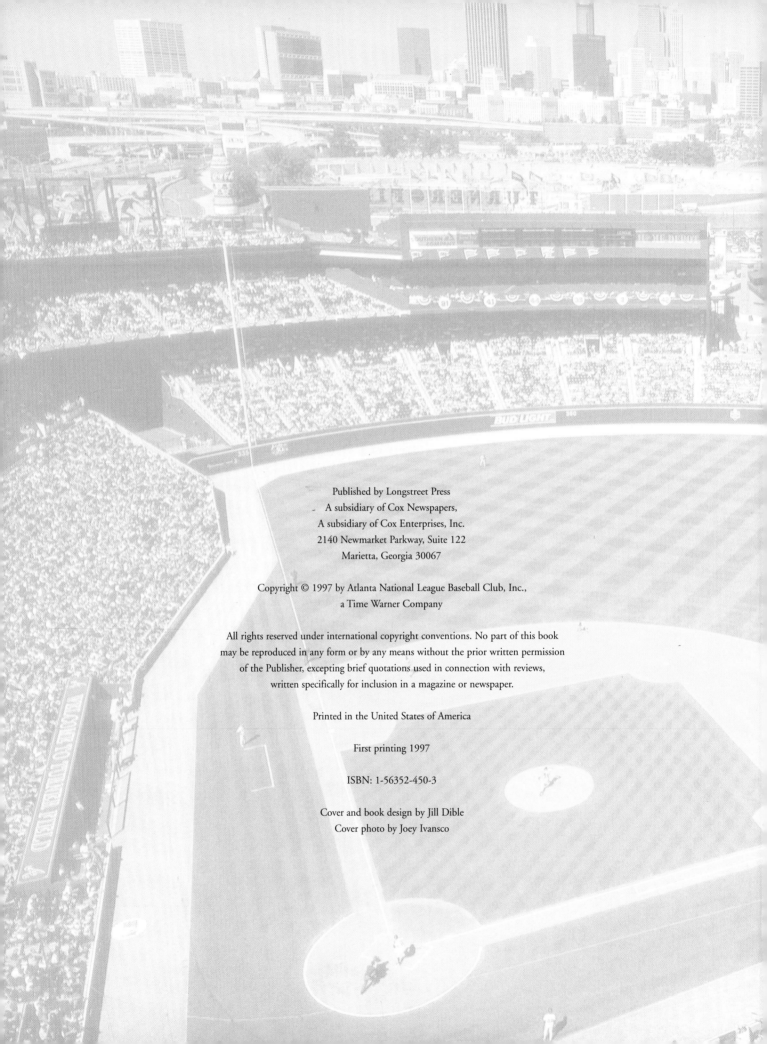

Published by Longstreet Press
A subsidiary of Cox Newspapers,
A subsidiary of Cox Enterprises, Inc.
2140 Newmarket Parkway, Suite 122
Marietta, Georgia 30067

Printed in the United States of America

First printing 1997

ISBN: 1-56352-450-3

Cover and book design by Jill Dible
Cover photo by Joey Ivansco

TABLE OF CONTENTS

In a pre-game ceremony on Sept. 15, 1997, Ted Turner presents Braves fans Jimmy and Rosalynn Carter an autographed jersey to commemorate the 15th anniversary of the Carter Presidential Center.

FOREWORD

As a farm boy, I grew up immersed in baseball. My first team effort was playing hardball with other boys in our rural Archery community. Without a screen behind home plate and with habitually wild and hard-throwing pitchers, I often had one of the most difficult positions, as the catcher's "backstop" — one of three white boys on a team of ten. I always wanted to pitch at school, encouraged and taught by my father Earl, who was on the mound every weekend for the American Legion team in our county seat.

Our family made the long trip to Atlanta about once a year, with the exciting dual destinations of the regional Sears-Roebuck headquarters (where catalog items were delivered immediately!) and the Atlanta Crackers ballfield just across Ponce de Leon Avenue.

Daddy and my uncle were deeply involved in the management of the Class D Georgia-Florida league and rarely missed a game played in Americus. Usually after crops were laid by, they and their wives spent vacations in a different major league city each year: New York, Saint Louis, Chicago, Detroit, Cincinnati, Philadelphia, or wherever there would be the maximum number of games played during the ten days or so they could spend away from home.

They went to see Jackie Robinson play in 1947, which made my mother Lillian an avid Dodgers fan for life — even after the Braves moved to Atlanta in 1966. During her final years, she watched or listened to the West Coast games on special TV and radio systems and often called Tommy Lasorda personally to criticize his management decisions. When Mama died, we found a complete Dodgers uniform in her closet — from cap to cleats.

As a state senator, I watched the Braves' stadium being erected during a special legislative session when we were trying to write a new constitution for Georgia, and I was relieved and delighted when the Braves came to Atlanta. One of Ted Turner's earliest promises when he bought the Braves was that I would throw out the first ball at the World Series when his team became National League champions. He kept his pledge many years later, and I was proud that my pre-game practice paid off and I threw a strike, electronically timed at 48 miles per hour. (I claimed it was a change-up.)

One of the highlights of my governor's years was being present when Hank Aaron hit his historic home run. I remember that the Atlanta community gave him a beautiful new Cadillac, but he and I made some of the worldwide encyclopedias with a photograph of my giving him a ten-dollar license plate: HR 715. Hank is still a true hero of mine, and I am delighted to see him honored in many ways in the new Turner Field.

A few years later, when I was Democratic nominee for President and waiting to begin my general

Sid Bream's slide to send the Braves to the '92 World Series is the most exciting sports moment Jimmy Carter has ever witnessed.

election campaign, my brother Billy and I had after-noon softball contests in Plains. I soft-pitched for a team of mostly Secret Service agents, and Billy pitched for a team of news reporters. He always insisted that the broad-shouldered six-foot-four-inch athletes emerging from jet airplanes at the county airport were really reporters, and I denied that we brought in temporary security personnel who hap-pened to have some semi-pro baseball experience.

Great crowds came to Plains that summer, and we sometimes had more spectators at our softball games than attended the Braves' games in Atlanta. One of the biggest events in our town's history was when the entire Braves team came down to visit us. Mama par-ticularly enjoyed having a long discussion with Bobby Cox about baseball strategy and tactics.

A lot of people ask me about the greatest sporting event I've ever witnessed. I've seen a lot, but the most exciting and memorable of all was Atlanta's final playoff victory in the ninth inning over the Pittsburgh Pirates to win the National League cham-pionship in 1992. To me, the heart-stopping win-ning play was typical of the spirit, courage, and abil-ity of the Braves' teams over the years.

No matter where we are, we always try to watch the Braves games, and to a significant degree my atti-tude toward life is affected by the results of the last game. It is a great pleasure and honor for us as Georgians to be associated with a team of true cham-pions and to be able to watch them at their wonder-ful new ballpark, Turner Field. It is no mystery why we find other equally committed Braves fans throughout the nation, and the world.

Jimmy Carter

39th President of the United States

The entry plaza is Turner Field's signature amenity and a favorite gathering place for fans of all ages.

INTRODUCTION

An Evening at Turner Field

'THE BEST PLACE EVER BUILT TO PLAY AND WATCH BASEBALL'

It's 4:39 on a rather typical summertime Thursday afternoon, and Turner Field is about to come alive.

The Phillies, buried in last place in the National League East, are in town. The entire series is dedicated to observing the 50th anniversary of Jackie Robinson breaking the color barrier in the majors, but the big celebration — when both teams will wear replica 1938 Negro Leagues uniforms — is still two days away.

There's really nothing special about June 26 except that it's the Braves' 35th home date at their new ballpark. And that is special enough.

The first pitch is three hours away, the seating areas of the park won't open for another hour, and the heat and humidity of an Atlanta summer have finally set in. Yet hundreds of fans of all ages and descriptions, a few even in wheelchairs, many decked out in their finest — Braves caps and T-shirts, of course — are primed to explore and experience their new shrine the moment the clock strikes 4:40 and the gates swing open.

"It's amazing to see the people waiting in line when the gates open. There's absolutely no reason for it, but they do it," says Braves president Stan Kasten.

Indeed, they do. And as they swarm into the plaza, the significance of the scope of this new Home of the Braves is apparent.

Some purists and traditionalists and cranky media members who scorn the business of baseball have scoffed at the "theme-park" aspect of Turner Field. They think the game needs to offer fans little more than a seat and a scorecard, and they believe baseball can prosper as it did in the '50s and '60s without cre-

The retired numbers in Monument Grove provide unique photo opportunities.

STEVE JEFFORDS

Fans can test their broadcasting skill in the Fantasy Play By Play Booth.

atively building its fan base among children and families.

And they've never seen the excitement and wonder on the faces of kids and adults as they burst into Turner Field.

Where to go first?

The Chop House? Scout's Alley? Coca-Cola Sky Field? The museum? The 10 free Sega baseball games behind the east pavilion? The Clubhouse Store? Taste of the Major Leagues to grab a Philly cheesesteak — in honor of the visiting team? Have a personal baseball card made? Or cut a tape as the broadcaster calling a great moment in Braves history? Stand over the outfield wall and watch practice, perhaps even getting an autograph from a pitcher working out in the bullpen? Watch another game on the video wall? Or just mill around the plaza,

MAX ANTON BIRNKAMMER

The Turner Field Band helps create the plaza's festive atmosphere.

soak up the atmosphere and watch people?

They do all that . . . and more. In the process, they experience major league baseball in a way fans in other cities have never known and in a manner that would have been as foreign to Braves fans a year ago as cheering for the Dodgers or any other visiting team. A day at the ol' ballpark has never before been like this.

Just ask Phil Niekro, the Braves' newest Hall of Famer who spent 18 years at Atlanta-Fulton County Stadium and still regards himself as a Braves fan of the highest order.

"I felt like I was in a different city (from Atlanta) when I walked into Turner Field," he said. "It just didn't feel like the Braves' stadium to me. It's first-class, no question about it. It doesn't get any better than that."

And Niekro's fellow Braves fans heartily endorse his opinion. On June 23, before the '97 schedule was half played, the club sold its three millionth ticket for Turner Field's inaugural season, guaranteeing no worse than the second-best annual attendance in franchise history (second to the "last great pennant race" in 1993).

There is so much to the Turner Field experience that many fans get started even before the plaza opens three hours prior to game time. Monument Grove, a picturesque, non-ticketed area adjacent to the plaza on the north side of the park, invites fans no matter how early they arrive.

Two magnolia trees greet visitors there and provide a permanent tribute to old Ponce de Leon Park, where the Crackers were Atlanta's pro team for years and a grand magnolia actually was in play in center

Sluggers show off their swings in the Braves-themed batting cages located in Scout's Alley.

MAX ANTON BIRNKAMMER

The ball Hank Aaron hit for his record 715th home run hovers over the plaza and the Braves Clubhouse store.

field. Families picnic on the tables provided, and amateur photographers have a field day capturing their companions mugging at the many monuments or in front of the pennant wall on the back of the west pavilion.

Then, with the gates finally open, the action heats up quickly in the plaza where the brick facade of the ballpark and the green pavilion roofs provide a classic old-time feel, accentuated by the colorful, carnival-like concession, direction and attraction signs. Bright yellow flags, adorned with the red Braves' "A", flap in the breeze, and the 100-foot high blowup of Hank Aaron's 715th home run ball dominates the scene.

A four-man combo provides live music in front of the Clubhouse Store, and the rest of the Turner Field Band marches through Scout's Alley, playing loudly and stirring up a festive atmosphere for the evening. Braves mascots and Cartoon Network characters such as Scooby Doo, Yogi Bear and Fred Flintstone mingle with the crowd.

Within an hour, the Chop House is full, and it stays that way all night, fans waiting in line to sample a matchless dining experience — watching live major league baseball at the same time they're enjoying the restaurant's signature barbecue. It's a Turner Field exclusive.

So, too, are Scout's Alley and Coca-Cola Sky Field.

A long bank of televisions in the plaza shows every major league game being broadcast at any given moment.

At Scout's Alley, fans learn about what it takes to be a big leaguer and how talent scouts comb the sandlots of America and the world in search of the next Braves superstars. A true one-of-its-kind attraction developed for Turner Field, Scout's Alley allows fans to read actual scouting reports compiled about their favorite players when they were still in high school or college. At the same time, people can get an appreciation for the skills of a baseball professional by using and observing interactive exhibits and even batting and throwing in game simulators. Best of all, perhaps, is the fact that everything is Braves specific.

Turner Field was designed not just to give fans the ultimate baseball experience, but to give them the ultimate Braves experience.

Way above Scout's Alley, on the left-field roof, is Coca-Cola Sky Field, where a lucky fan might someday win $1 million . . . and where any fan at any game can get an up-close look at the 42-foot contour bottle decorated like a giant all-Braves Christmas tree, cool off at a misting station, and visit several other attractions while enjoying a sky-line view of the ballgame and the city.

Now, it's becoming obvious why so many fans get to Turner Field so early — there really is so much to do . . . too much to do in just one trip to 755 Hank Aaron Drive.

Modern technology allows lucky fans to interview players before each game on the plaza video board.

And wherever fans are as 6:30 approaches (or one hour, 10 minutes before game time), they start circulating back to the plaza in front of the Clubhouse Store for yet another Turner Field exclusive — the Braves player interview.

Turner Field was designed to bring the fans closer to the game in every way, including this opportunity for fans to actually talk to a player through the wonders of modern telecommunications.

Five fans are selected in advance to ask questions to a specific player. When the big moment arrives, the fan and player come "face to face" in the plaza. Even though the player is physically in the clubhouse, he appears live on the giant video board on the back of the scoreboard. The fan asks a question directly to the player, and the player answers right back. It's teleconferencing, Braves style.

An hour until game time. Whew! There's still time to have a collage made of photos from the Braves archives . . . or to have a customized picture made of a great moment in Braves history — with you right in the midst of it. Be a part of Sid Bream's winning slide in the '92 NLCS. Your friends back home might be a little suspicious, but who cares.

And, don't forget to take the kids to Tooner Field where there are pint-sized tables, chairs, counters and even concessions, decorated with colorful cartoon images — in a baseball setting, of course.

Before long, a Braves game actually breaks out. With all seats angled toward the center of the play-

With seats located close to the field and angled toward the action, there's not a better place to watch baseball.

ing field and as close to the action as allowed by law, there's not a better place to watch it. But for those fans who don't like to sit still long or who just can't get enough of exploring Turner Field, continued browsing is permitted. In fact, it can be done literally without missing a pitch.

The wide terrace level concourse is completely open to the field, allowing fans to walk the ballpark while watching the game. Many choose to hang over the bullpens, the Braves' in right field and the visitor's in left, or to watch from the two-level Chop House.

Televisions are everywhere, too, and that includes the plaza, where a remarkable number of fans continue to congregate throughout the game. They eat, shop and play games while keeping up with the action on the video board. Or, using the plaza as an open-air living room, they simply sit on the brick pavement and watch the Braves on the big screen and all the other games in progress on the long bank of smaller TVs.

Even after the final out of the game, many fans remain, taking in all Turner Field has to offer for the hour the ballpark remains open. Eventually, the plaza grows quiet again, only as fans are left no choice but to head for home or their hotel room. But, like magic, they return again the next afternoon at 4:40, and the whole scenario repeats itself.

Turner Field . . . Kasten calls it: "The best place ever built to play and watch baseball."

Turner Field . . . It's the rarest of diamonds.

Turner Field is all aglow for its official coming out party on April 4, 1997.

THE FIRST GAME

SOME ENCHANTED EVENING

It was an evening like no other in franchise history. Oh, sure, the Braves had opened new ball-parks before — Braves Field in Boston in 1915 . . . Milwaukee County Stadium in 1953 . . . and Atlanta Stadium in 1966.

Well, the last one wasn't actually new. The minor league Crackers broke in Atlanta Stadium in 1965, while the Braves remained in Wisconsin one more season due to legalities. But the team's first game in the South certainly was a major event, even if there already were more than a few wads of gum stuck on the undersides of the seats and the ballclub was well past its Milwaukee glory days.

The opening of Braves Field in Boston was monumental because it unveiled the largest ballpark in the majors at the time. It took place the year after the "Miracle" Braves pulled off a stunning World Series championship, but came in August when it was apparent only another miracle — one that didn't transpire — would produce a pennant.

As for the Wisconsin debut, Milwaukee was astir over its new-found big league status, but hopes for the team were unnecessarily yet understandably low since the '52 Braves finished seventh in their New England swan song.

Turner Field's coming-out party on April 4, 1997, had it all.

Braves fans not only welcomed a brand new ball-park (okay, so there were a few races and a little fire ceremony there the previous summer), but they also got to revel in the moment with the defending National League champs who were big favorites to return to the World Series for the fifth time in seven years.

In many ways, it was an occasion that more than any other symbolized the Braves' meteoric rise from the scrap heap of baseball to the heights of the game, with the exception of the night the '95 World Series was won. The magnitude of Turner Field's opening was a memorable event of its own, but the Braves added unforgettable magic to the occasion with dramatic pregame ceremonies, a tight ballgame, and in the end, the perfect climax — a satisfying come-from-behind victory over the Cubs.

It was almost as if the whole performance was scripted by the baseball gods. If anyone didn't believe the night was heavenly inspired when the all-time home run king strolled in through the center field gate clutching home plate from Atlanta-Fulton County Stadium or when Whitney Houston's backup singers from the movie *The Preacher's Wife* performed the national anthem, they surely were convinced when a feathered spirit from the right-field sky swooped in to land at home plate on the anthem's final note.

Sheer enchantment.

John Smoltz (l) and Chipper Jones prepare to open the doors.

The evening began with Braves players opening the gates for anxious fans. Commemorative tickets, embossed but not torn, free lapel pins and foam tomahawks, and special "First Game" programs helped put everyone in a party frame of mind.

Billy Payne, the man who brought the Olympics to Atlanta, turned over the ballpark's keys to Braves president Stan Kasten. The Braves got their National League championship rings. Hank Aaron, completing the relay of home plate from the old ballpark to the new one, strolled in to thunderous applause. He was met at the pitcher's mound by Tom Glavine, a cornerstone of the new Braves era, and the two placed the familiar platter in place. The Georgia Mass Choir sang, and America's only trained bald eagle — Challenger — punctuated the anthem with a perfectly timed landing. Ted Turner threw out the ceremonial first pitch. Then the ballgame began, with historians and appreciative fans taking note of the bevy of Turner Field "firsts."

Denny Neagle threw the first "first" to Cubs batter Brian McRae, who promptly bunted it to Fred McGriff for an out. A low-key first pitch, perhaps, but an efficient one.

The Cubs cooperated nicely, three up and three down, affording fan favorite Chipper Jones the honor of stroking the first hit, a clean single to left with two outs in the bottom of the first.

With the game still scoreless in the bottom of the third, Braves newcomer Michael Tucker lined a pitch from Cubs starter Kevin Foster into the right-field seats for a 1-0 lead and a prominent position on the "firsts" ledger. Turner Field's history was unfolding in a hurry, and with a decidedly agreeable Braves flavor.

However, the visitors from Chicago weren't so accommodating after all. In fact, they carried a 4-2 advantage into the bottom of the seventh, forcing the faithful to ponder the most discouraging of Turner Field "firsts" — a defeat.

In the end, though, the stage had just been set for the most favorable of endings — a come-from-behinder. The Braves got one run in the seventh and two in the eighth for a 5-4 victory, the decisive run scoring when Chipper Jones notched his third hit of the proceedings.

Chip, Chip, Hooray! Turner Field was christened in a manner befitting its majestic presence.

ATLANTA BRAVES

The Georgia Mass Choir, fresh off their appearance in the motion picture The Preacher's Wife, *sings the national anthem at the opener.*

CHRIS HAMILTON

Challenger touches down on Al Cecere precisely at 'and the home of the brave.'

IT MUST HAVE BEEN HEAVEN-SENT

CHALLENGER'S STATS

AGE: **9**

WINGSPAN: **6** FEET

WEIGHT: **7** POUNDS

TALON GRIP: **1,000** LBS. OF PRESSURE PER SQ. FT.

Probably the toughest critics viewing the "First Game" ceremonies at Turner Field were the players themselves. They get around a lot, you know, and see about every sort of festivity that can be devised for a ballpark — indoors or out, in the U.S. and Canada and occasionally at exhibitions in other nations.

Fireworks, celebrities, gimmicks, presentations . . . they've seen it all . . . but never before anything like what they saw April 4, 1997.

Years from now, when time has eroded their mem-

ories and ours of exactly what happened that evening, one stirring image will remain, focused and precise, as if it occurred yesterday — the eagle.

Tom Glavine knows: "The eagle was absolutely fantastic. Everyone was amazed. It was awesome in size and the way it landed like that."

"You talk about chills and goose bumps!" said Denny Neagle, the starting pitcher that night. "I was just trying to focus on what I had to do, but how do you keep your concentration when you see something like that?"

Even Al Cecere knows he witnessed sheer magic, and he's the man who made it happen (though he defers all credit to a higher being).

"I said at the time that God choreographed it, and I still believe that," said Cecere, who operates the National Foundation to Protect America's Eagles at the Dollywood theme park in Pigeon Forge, Tennessee.

With the Georgia Mass Choir singing the national

anthem, Cecere's eagle swooped in from the Skyline seats in right field, circled and preened over the infield as the anthem wound down, then dramatically landed on his trainer's arm exactly when the performers finished . . . "the brave."

Location may be everything in real estate and pitching, but timing is everything in performing. To that end, the eagle named in honor of the lost Challenger astronauts put on a flawless show.

Cecere's explanation for his "partner's" genius: "Challenger thinks he's human."

"He's an unusual bird," added Cecere, who has dedicated his last 14 years to saving and protecting eagles. "When Challenger was a very young chick, he was blown out of his nest. The people who found him raised him. When that happens to a bird of prey in its first two weeks, it becomes a human imprint. It thinks the people are its parents and that it's a person."

Cecere's organization keeps only disabled eagles. Healthy ones are released into the wild. Challenger is handicapped only by his human side — the very thing that makes him trainable. Cecere uses age-old falconry techniques based on positive reinforcement, in the form of food, to train Challenger.

"You could never take a (normal) young bird and train him like that," said Cecere. "But Challenger has had too much human contact. Each time he's been released, he's landed near people looking for food. The third time, a man tried to beat him with a stick but was stopped by another man who turned him over to us. Everyone knows Challenger could not survive in the wild."

And so this physically perfect creation of nature, limited mentally because he thinks he's one of us, remains in captivity to thrill us.

"It's been a dream of mine for a long time to groom him to fly during the national anthem," said Cecere. "I've been grooming him little by little."

Several rehearsals preceded Challenger's Turner Field flight. At the big moment, handlers took the eagle to his right-field Skyline perch in a large travel carrier so his performance would remain a surprise to all. He was kept hooded until takeoff, then was left to depart on his own, the attraction of Cecere's whistle and the lure of dinner awaiting below.

Congratulations followed from some impressive fronts.

"Ted Turner came up and said, 'Fantastic. You did a great job'," Cecere recalled. "And Jimmy Carter offered Challenger a peanut. It was a memorable night, a dream come true."

THE FIRST PITCH CATCHER

Mike Mordecai is a bit player. Mostly, he sits in the background for the superstar-laden Braves. He pinch-hits, plays a little as a reserve infielder, and serves as the team's "emergency catcher." He even endured a demotion to the Braves' Richmond farm team in Turner Field's inaugural season. His moments to shine are few and far between, but he's exhibited a knack for taking advantage of opportunity when it presents itself.

On April 4, 1997, there was a loud knock at Mordecai's door, and the result was an evening that will always rank near the top on his list of personal highlights in the major leagues.

In 1995, Mordecai's first full season in the majors, he latched onto a secondary job as the player assigned to catch the ceremonial first pitch thrown by a politician, celebrity, civic leader . . . whoever happened to have the honor prior to each game. Generally, it's a relatively mundane task for a major leaguer, but it's one Mordecai came to enjoy — and to protect. When it was suggested he relinquish the duty after two years, he balked.

Reserve infielder Mike Mordecai (l) had the honor of receiving Ted Turner's ceremonial first pitch.

"If I was playing every day, I'd give it up," he said. "But since I'm not, I wanted to keep it."

Thus, it was the 29-year-old reserve who had the honor of being the "receiver" of Ted Turner's ceremonial first pitch to open the ballpark named in his honor.

"Ted's really an electric type person . . . it's like there's electricity coming off him," said Mordecai. "I said, 'Ted, what do you want to throw, a fastball or a slider?' And he said, 'I just want to get it to the plate.' I said, 'I'm sure you will,' and he threw it right over the middle.

"I gave Ted the ball, and (team photographer) Walter (Victor) took a picture of us together. I signed the ball, although I thought of asking Ted to sign it for me. But with all he's done for the Braves and Atlanta, I just didn't think I should do that. There couldn't be a better owner in baseball."

Turner, by the way, kept the ball and has it at his home.

"I've got an 8 x 10 of the picture that my wife (Susie) had framed for our home," Mordecai said. "I don't usually get things signed, but I've been thinking about bringing it in and asking Ted to sign it. It would be nice some day to sit back and look at it, knowing that it's signed by the man the ballpark is named after and who threw out the first pitch to me."

Many games, the first-ball ceremony is as close as Mordecai gets to seeing action. But that was not the case on April 4, 1997.

The Braves were trailing the Cubs, 4-3, in the bottom of the eighth and were in danger of losing a game that will always have a prominent place in franchise history. With Jeff Blauser at first and one out, Mordecai was called on to pinch-hit for reliever Brad Clontz, and he responded with a clutch single to left. Blauser later scored to tie the game, and Mordecai eventually rode home on Chipper Jones'

two-out single for what proved to be the decisive run in Turner Field's inaugural game.

"I really didn't think too much about scoring the winning run at the time," Mordecai said. "Driving home after the game, I started to think about it a little. But I don't look at it that way — as being the winning run — because we needed all five runs to win. I did help us win, though, and that's always a good feeling, especially on a night like that."

All in all, it was quite a night for the bit player from Birmingham.

"First of all, it was the opening of a new ballpark," he said. "I was part of a group of guys making a new beginning here. With the type of franchise we have — all the winning in the '90s — opening a new ballpark was something very special. In 30 or 40 years, I can bring my grandkids to Turner Field and say, 'I played here Opening Night.'

"It was just a magnificent evening for me all the way around. To be the catcher for Ted Turner . . . Hank Aaron and Tom Glavine bringing in home plate . . . then getting to play and score the winning run. Those are some pretty good memories.

"I was just in the right place at the right time, but I'm awfully glad I was."

Is that "Tucker" Field?

Michael Tucker's arrival in Atlanta was not all that welcomed. The fans didn't have anything personal against the speedy young outfielder. It's just that the Braves had to part with Jermaine Dye, a young outfielder who'd acquitted himself well, to acquire Tucker in the spring of '97 from Kansas City.

But Tucker quickly won the support of the masses with his play, including the first home run at Turner Field.

ALLISON SHIRREFFS

Braves newcomer Michael Tucker baptizes Turner Field with its first home run.

CHRIS HAMILTON

Fan favorite Chipper Jones shows plenty of sock for the opener.

Fans wondered who would strike the most memorable of "firsts" at the new ballpark. Would it be Klesko, McGriff, Chipper or Andruw, Lopez? Few probably considered Tucker as the likely slugger, but then that's how unpredictable baseball is.

With one out and no one on base in the bottom of the third inning, the left-handed hitter slammed a first-pitch changeup from Cubs starter Kevin Foster into the right-field seats.

"I didn't really think about the fact that it was the first home run at Turner Field when I hit it or when I was running around the bases," said Tucker. "Then I got back to the dugout and said,

'Wow!' It just didn't set in right away that, hey, this is a new park, and that's the first home run here."

A season ticket holder, Chuck Austin from Kings Mountain, North Carolina, caught the ball. He loaned it to the Ivan Allen Jr. Braves Museum and Hall of Fame so all Turner Field visitors would have a chance to see it.

THE PEOPLE'S CHOICE

If Braves fans could have voted on who would get the first hit at Turner Field, their choice most likely would have been Chipper Jones. Of course, no such

Denny Neagle's first pitch results in an out . . . and a misplaced piece of history.

poll was taken, but as fate would have it, the immensely popular third baseman put himself in the record books and thrilled his legions of fans with a two-out single to left in the bottom of the first inning.

"It meant a lot to me," Jones said of his first-pitch hit off Cubs starter Kevin Foster. "Everyone wants to know that kind of stuff . . . first hit, first walk, first stolen base . . ."

And then he grinned, knowing well that he also got the first walk (third inning) and the first stolen base (seventh inning). That's not to mention the first game-winning hit (a two-out single in the eighth).

"I hit a first-pitch fastball," he said in elaborating on the first hit. "Foster throws a lot of changeups, but it was the first inning, first pitch, so I was looking for a fastball. At first, I thought the leftfielder was going to catch it. It was a special moment. I told (first base coach) Pat (Corrales) to get the ball."

The ball? Jones promptly had it signed by Ted Turner and took it home to display in his personal shrine. The Braves, however, had other ideas and asked him to loan it for display in the Ivan Allen Jr. Braves Museum.

"I hope I get it back someday," Jones said, shaking his head and showing that grin that helped make the first hit at Turner Field the people's choice.

ONE THAT GOT AWAY

Chipper Jones got the ball from his first hit at Turner Field. A fan got the ball from Michael Tucker's first home run at the park. But no one knows where the ball is that Denny Neagle used to throw the first pitch.

If it had been simply a ball or a strike, perhaps someone would have thought to throw it out of the game for safekeeping. But since Cubs leadoff man Brian McRae put it in play as a bunt to first baseman Fred McGriff for an unassisted putout, apparently no one thought to save it.

"I don't know what happened to the ball," Neagle said. "No one ever yelled to throw it in. After Freddie made the out, they just threw it around the infield, and when it came back to me, no one asked for it, and I didn't think about it. It probably wound up being used in batting practice the next day, or it's in the hands of some fan who doesn't even realize it was the first ball thrown at Turner Field."

Actually, it's the former. The same ball was used for the entire top half of the first inning, according to Glen Serra, the Braves' media relations manager. When it was thrown out in the middle of the inning, Serra called the dugout and asked bench coach Jim Beauchamp to save it. However, before Beauchamp got word to the ballboy, the ball was thrown into a bag with several others for recycling as batting practice fodder. A piece of history had slipped through the Braves' fingers.

Neagle was pleased to have the honor of being the "First Game" pitcher, though he admitted, "It was just the luck of the draw."

The Braves opened the season with three games in Houston where the more-decorated John Smoltz, Greg Maddux and Tom Glavine worked. Neagle said he realized early in the spring he was on schedule to pitch the first game at Turner Field but thought Bobby Cox might alter plans due to the significance of the ballpark's opening.

"I didn't know if Bobby would change things so that Tommy, who's been here the longest, or Smoltzie, who won the Cy Young Award last year, could pitch," Neagle said. "But I knew if it worked out for me, I'd sure take it. Games like that are special. You know you'll be a part of history. Forty or 50 years from now, they'll be asking, 'Who threw the first pitch at Turner Field?', and my name will come up."

A view from the north shows the plaza, Monument Grove and the Braves executive offices where there once was part of the oval of the Olympic stadium.

THE MAKING OF
TURNER FIELD

It began with Billy Payne's dream, developed in Stan Kasten's vision, and stands today at 755 Hank Aaron Drive as both an enduring reminder of the glory of the summer of '96 and as the magnificent Home of the Braves.

That Turner Field is indeed the Rarest of Diamonds among America's baseball parks is a credit to hundreds of people who worked countless hours to make magic from concrete, steel and brick. But above all, it is a monument to Payne's landmark achievement of bringing the Centennial Olympic Games to Atlanta and to Kasten's foresight to create a ballpark unlike any other that would provide legions of fans with the ultimate cathedral in which to celebrate their devotion to the most successful baseball team of modern times.

Just goes to show what can be made of a paper napkin.

Yes, the story of Turner Field began on a common paper napkin, according to Payne, who as an Atlanta attorney devised the grand plan for hosting the world for the 1996 Summer Games.

"I know the exact moment the idea (for a new stadium) came to me in the spring of 1987," said Payne, who became president and CEO of the Atlanta Committee for the Olympic Games and now serves as vice-chairman of NationsBank. "It was within 60 days of the original idea to go after the Games when we were first dealing with making an inventory of the assets and venues we had available and matching them to our limited knowledge of what it would take to host the Games.

"One thing we had to deal with early was the biggest and most obvious. Literally, on a napkin I drew a sketch of a circle that represented the existing (Atlanta-Fulton County) stadium. And I drew an oval on what was the big parking lot on the south side of the stadium. The theory was to build there

Billy Payne participated in the Opening Night festivities.

Braves president Stan Kasten (r) and ACOG's A.D. Frazier (l) had plenty of reason to smile when ground was finally broken.

because we wouldn't need to acquire additional property, which would save money. I thought immediately that we could somehow convert this oval into a new baseball stadium, though I had no idea if the technology existed to do that.

"At that time, it was fairly high in the consciousness of the community that if we didn't build a stadium for the Braves, they'd move to the suburbs. It all coincided.

"I was sitting in my car somewhere. I used to keep a supply of paper napkins in the glove compartment, and multiple times I made sketches on one of those while I was driving."

Making a crude drawing on a napkin is one thing. Convincing people that what's on that piece of paper can become the major facility for the world's largest sporting event — and then serve as the home of a major league baseball team . . . well, that's something else. This is especially true when the most recent

example of such an undertaking is generally regarded as a dismal failure. That is Montreal's Olympic Stadium. A venue for the 1980 Summer Games that became the home of the Expos, it is considered an inferior place to play and watch baseball.

That's not what Kasten, the Braves' president, was interested in seeing his ballclub stuck with. And fortunately, it's not what Payne wanted to leave behind as a legacy of his impact on history. It just took some doing for him to convince everyone — Olympic officials, architects, the Braves — that his plan would work.

As much as Kasten wanted a new ballpark for the Braves, his knowledge of the Montreal situation made him leery of Payne's proposal. An oval stadium built for track and field just wasn't conducive to baseball. And the idea to somehow convert the oval into a conventional baseball park was, to say the least, a little out in left field.

ALLISON SHIRREFFS

The Braves brought in Janet Marie Smith from Baltimore's Camden Yards to head their design team.

"I remember Billy coming into my office and telling me what he had in mind," recalled Kasten. "I have to admit I was more than a little bit skeptical."

That was in the spring of 1988 when Payne was preparing the presentation to the U.S. Olympic Committee that he hoped would result in Atlanta becoming the USOC's "bid city," thus clearing the way for making a proposal to the International Olympic Committee.

"There was great pessimism in the architectural community initially about our ability to convert it efficiently," said Payne. "I remember as the months progressed and we got into the first drawing, we were showing it was possible to do the conversion at a time when the experts said we couldn't.

"To me, it seemed easy to build a baseball stadium and supplement the balance of the oval with temporary stuff that looks like it's permanent. I wasn't a bit smarter (than the architects), but I was persistent. I

knew what I've always known — that where there's a will, there's a way."

Indeed, there was.

"Architects are much better marketers than people give them credit for," Payne said. "They never told me it was impossible, because they knew I'd eliminate them from my list if they did. I think the corner was turned when they got into it and started dealing with an inventory of the site, the resources, the budget, etc.

"Sure, it would have been infinitely easier to just build an Olympic stadium, but only an idiot would assume there would be a need for an 85,000-seat stadium for anything other than the Olympics. Some folks have criticized an Olympic stadium being used for baseball, saying it's sacrilegious. But we weren't about to build a facility for a one-time purpose. What we did was logical as well as helpful, to convert it into something the community needed for the future."

Chuck Winstead (l) of Beers Construction and Turner's Bunky Helfrich were key figures in making Turner Field come together on time.

The USOC, of course, sanctioned Payne's plan, and on September 18, 1990, IOC president Juan Antonio Samaranch announced that Atlanta had been chosen to host the Centennial Olympic Games. For a very brief moment, time stood still for Payne and his cohorts on the Atlanta Olympic Organizing Committee. But the clock started ticking immediately toward July 19, 1996, Atlanta's date with its Olympic destiny.

At the same time, the Braves were wrapping up yet another miserable season as the worst team in baseball. John Schuerholz was still employed by the Kansas City Royals, and Terry Pendleton was a St. Louis Cardinal. Yet the reality in the Braves' cramped offices at Atlanta-Fulton County Stadium was that franchise history had just been altered, too. The team would have a new home — at no cost — for the 1997 season. Little did anyone realize just what the ensuing six years would bring, though.

LAYING THE GROUNDWORK

Securing the bid to host the 1996 Olympics was a major accomplishment in itself, but it was only the start in the long and difficult struggle to bring the new Olympic stadium — and eventually Turner Field — to life. In fact, it took nearly three years, until July 10, 1993, just to break ground on the old Red Zone parking lot south of Atlanta-Fulton County Stadium where Payne first sketched the oval on his rough napkin plan.

For Kasten and A.D. Frazier, Payne's right-hand man as the COO at ACOG, it was three years of hell.

Kasten and Frazier were mere acquaintances when they came together to lay the groundwork for construction by working the politicians and cutting the myriad of deals it would take to spend $207 million of ACOG's money and another $45 million of Braves money (some $15 million of which was fronted by Aramark, the concessionaire at Turner Field, as a tradeoff against percentages that would be owed the team on future sales at the ballpark). But by the time ground was broken, the two executives had survived a number of heated discussions and mini-crises to form a strong bond and a great deal of respect for each other.

"My memories of building Turner Field start with 18 months of making deals and another 18 months to get an agreement," Kasten said. "It was so stressful. I was taking the hits for everything, but I knew it was a special thing. The labor, the pain, was very difficult, but the child is wonderful and getting better all the time."

There were many days when the two wondered how the project would ever get started, let alone completed in time. And there were times when they didn't even know where it would be built.

"I never worked so hard to give away a $207 million stadium in my life," said Frazier, now president and CEO of Invesco, Inc., in Atlanta.

Rather than building the stadium where Payne envisioned it and where it now sits, Frazier said he originally wanted to put it east of Capitol Avenue (now Hank Aaron Drive) and north of Ralph David Abernathy Boulevard on another parking lot site owned by the Atlanta-Fulton County Recreation Authority. He felt it would have been a better location for several reasons, including the fact that it would sit up higher and have a better view of downtown. However, the city rejected the idea because it felt there would be too much disruption to the neighborhood, even though ACOG offered to relocate any homeowners who were displaced, just as it did on the current site.

As time pressed on, Frazier continued to have difficulty reaching an agreement with the city on a location for the stadium. With contractors anxious to go to work for fear of not being able to complete the pro-

Henry Teague was the project architect.

ject on time, Frazier began to look at other options.

"We came within 24 hours of building it on 170 acres outside Atlanta in the north suburbs," he said. "Between the city, the county and the recreation authority, I felt we weren't going to be able to close the deal. So, I bought an option on some land. It didn't cost much. Stan would've moved there. That's a fact. It was difficult getting all parties with their oars in the water at the same time. It was a terrible time. But finally, the city council adopted the plan for the current site, though they did so with some rancor."

FIRST THINGS FIRST

All the while, what became known as the Atlanta Stadium Design Team (ASDT) was being assembled and going about the task of mapping out exactly how the stadium/ballpark would look and how such

ATLANTA BRAVES

This maze of concrete and steel became Turner Field.

a major undertaking, the likes of which had never before been attempted, would be executed.

A collaboration of companies, ASDT included four architectural firms as its chief players. Heery International was in charge of managing the entire project. Ellerbe Becket, a Kansas City-based firm that has designed many major sports facilities, did the original schematic plan for Atlanta's Olympic stadium that was used in Payne's proposal to the USOC. Rosser International was the project architect, responsible for the ultimate design of the stadium and its transformation into Turner Field. And Williams Russell and Johnson provided civil engineering design and worked with Rosser on structural engineering. Also in the mix from the start was Beers Construction, the general contractor.

For the Braves, the key players were Kasten; Janet Marie Smith, the architect and urban planner recruited from Baltimore after her role in designing

Oriole Park at Camden Yards; Bunky Helfrich, president of Turner Properties; John Schuerholz, the team's general manager; and Bob Wolfe, the club's senior vice-president of administration.

"Shortly after the announcement that Atlanta got the Olympics, we got together and hired an architectural firm (Ellerbe) and a contractor (Beers)," said Helfrich, a lifelong friend of Ted Turner's, who sailed with Turner in his successful America's Cup defense in 1977 and was in charge of building the original CNN headquarters on Techwood Drive in 1979-80.

"We wanted to make sure we got a baseball stadium. Ellerbe Beckett did the schematic design. We reviewed it internally, and Beers priced it out. The appearance changed, but not the basic design, and we established a budget. We gave that information to ACOG, and they had it for about a year. They selected the same designer and massaged the budget. It was $225 million, but ACOG got it down to $207 million. Initially, we came up with a futuristic design. We couldn't afford the 'flying' roof, but what we were all interested in was the major part of the design for baseball."

From the start, ACOG committed to design a baseball park first, build its Olympic stadium with a modified design, then retrofit to the original baseball design.

"If not for that forethought, we wouldn't have been a part of it," said Helfrich. "It's a credit to Billy Payne and ACOG."

In doing their homework, Kasten and Helfrich went to Baltimore to tour Camden Yards, which opened in 1992. The person who showed them around happened to be Smith, who'd just been through with the Orioles what the Braves were plunging into. Not only that, but her work had won rave reviews.

"Stan suggested we see if we could hire her for our stadium," Helfrich said. "We had lots of conversations and finally were successful. We felt like John Schuerholz, organizing the team and getting the best players we could. Janet was the No.-1 draft pick.

"She's a very, very talented person and well-tuned to the baseball business. Her product at Camden, at the time, was the best in baseball. We knew of her experience doing that stadium, but we didn't realize all the qualities she had at the time."

As it turned out, Smith was the perfect fit for the job. Experienced, knowledgeable and hard-working, she was able to fuse her own ideas with Kasten's perception of what the ballpark should be.

"Make no mistake, this was Stan's vision from the beginning," said Wolfe, who was in charge of operational issues. "He was the one who looked at the ideas and design and knew almost immediately: This is what we want or need or don't want or don't need.

"Janet presented and developed a lot of ideas, but all with Stan's vision. She is the most detailed person I've ever worked with. No issue is too small. She spent hours and hours on things so minute that others wouldn't bother with them. There's not one single part of the park that she broadstroked. Time was never an issue with her."

It was Smith and Helfrich who directed design for the Braves.

"We designed a baseball park, then converted it to an Olympic stadium on paper, and then back again," said Smith. "It was a very frightening thing to be doing when all the barometers suggested it couldn't be done — Montreal and being in the same era as (acclaimed new ballparks) Coors (Denver), Jacobs (Cleveland), Camden (Baltimore). Making a ballpark that was functional and had such a radically different purpose was very hard."

Much of the design came from Kasten's perception of what he wanted the ballpark to be. First and foremost, he wanted it to be a fan's park, not only a place where people would have an unsurpassed view

of the ballgame, but also a place where they would want to come early and stay late to enjoy a host of modern amenities and diversions. He also wanted a ballpark that was more architecturally contemporary than the other so-called "retro" parks built in recent years, yet one that nevertheless possessed an old-time feel that would appeal to baseball traditionalists.

"The first thing in the process was the open concourse where you could walk the park and still see the game," Kasten said of the wide, unobstructed concourse behind the Terrace Level. "That alone was a difficult process but it was very important. As the geometry evolved, we saw we could put in the plaza. But the No.-1 thing was to have an intimate baseball field and seating with an open concourse. Then credit the design team for filling out and maximizing the space."

In Kasten's quest to give fans something to do before and after the game, the entry plaza was designed not only as a place for games and concessions, but also as an open area where people could congregate, mingle, and just plain watch each other.

"People ask me what I like most about the park, and they expect me to pick an object," said Smith. "But I like the void, the space, the plaza. The most memorable places are spaces, not objects. The plaza pulls you into the park."

The initial design of the plaza was done by Ayers/Saint/Gross of Baltimore, who did a study of some of the world's best-known open spaces, including St. Peter's Square at the Vatican, in developing its drawings for the Braves.

In the serious baseball areas, such as the dimensions of the park and the layout of the clubhouse, Schuerholz and Dean Taylor, his assistant general manager, were heavily involved in design. One of the most interesting things to come out of their work is the unique shape of the Braves' clubhouse. Some have likened it to a keyhole because it's configured like a circle that's connected to a rectangle.

W.A. BRIDGES, JR.

Turner Field in its earlier incarnation.

"It's never been done before in major league baseball," Schuerholz said. "We were challenged by the location of two huge cement support columns in the area. This shape was suggested to us, and though we'd never seen anything like it before, the more we looked at it, the more we liked it. It turned out to be spectacular.

"In many of the new parks, the clubhouses are huge but linear so the players at one end can hardly communicate with those at the other end. But the majority of our players are in the circular area. They have plenty of space, but they're not so spread out that you lose the feeling of being together."

The challenges in sculpting this two-in-one facility were immense. Among other things, the Braves were in the midst of sudden, dramatic success that would have taxed their staff even without the addition of building a ballpark.

"One of the real challenges was that not only were

we still doing our daily business, but we were doing so in what were then atypical years for us," Wolfe said. "Our season ticket base went from 5,000 to 30,000, and the seasons were played well into October. It's not as if we could stop what we were doing and build this ballpark. It was in addition to what we already had on our plate."

And to achieve an end result that would please both ACOG and the Braves required some imaginative work, the most unique aspect of which was the "double-thinking" that was applied to virtually every part of the building.

"One of the things that made this project absolutely unique and exciting was that we almost had to design it backwards/forward," said Heery's George Taft, the project manager for ASDT.

"ACOG had a strong commitment to do a state-of-the-art Braves stadium while not compromising a state-of-the-art Olympic configuration. We were continually trying to balance the baseball design with what ACOG could live with for the Olympics.

"For example, on the club level, could ACOG live with the suites for their sponsors as the Braves wanted them? It turned out they could. But they couldn't when it came to other things. On the west side, ACOG needed a warm-up track under the building on the service level. For baseball, that area needed to be locker rooms for the visitors, officials and event staff. So, we had to design it so that the underground utilities, sanitation, etc., that would be needed after the Olympics were built early enough and in place for the Olympics even though they weren't needed then."

The need for such planning and construction was two-fold. First of all, it helped keep down the cost of the project. And secondly, there was very little time — seven months — to turn the Olympic stadium into the Home of the Braves in time for the opening of the 1997 season.

"The time from the closing of the Olympics and Paralympics to the opening of baseball was very compressed," Taft said. "In reality, that schedule was much more complicated and intense than the schedule for constructing the Olympic configuration.

"So, the decision was made to build everything we could for the Braves during the Olympic configuration. For example, all the underground utilities for the Braves and the piles necessary to hold up the baseball offices were put in under the track during the Olympic period. So, when we came back after the Olympics and ripped up the track, the bulldozer scratched the surface and found the pile caps we put in a year before to serve as the base for the columns that support the office building. It was like a dog burying a bone and coming back later and digging it up. We were digging for buried treasure. It was the key to rapid turnover. Because of that, the design for the final baseball stadium had

to be complete before the design for the Olympics.

"All that juxtaposition made this uniquely challenging. I don't know of any other building where this was done."

Another example is the scoreboard, which was originally installed in three horizontal sections for the Olympics. But it was designed so that it could be reconfigured for the Braves with the video board on top of the matrix board.

Many things, especially seats, were re-used or recycled. Though some temporary Olympic seats were sold after the Games, many of those in the north end that were removed to make room for the baseball configuration and the plaza were actually permanent seats that were relocated to outfield seating areas that didn't exist during the Olympics.

From ground breaking on July 10, 1993, contractors had just under three years to prepare for the Opening Ceremony of the Olympics on July 19, 1996. Actually, the facility was completed well in advance, enabling a trial run in May when the Atlanta Grand Prix was held there.

Along the way, the Braves, seeing the opportunity to create a ballpark that was beyond even their initial dreams, added amenities, including the plaza, that drove up the cost of the building considerably from ACOG's $207-million contribution. Frazier allowed them to be included in the design, even though he didn't have the money to pay the bills — just Kasten's word that it would be forthcoming.

"I went long on Stan for $34 million," Frazier said. "He gave me his word in May of 1995 that Turner would put in an additional $30-35 million. Nothing was signed, but like everything else he said to me, he delivered. That's extraordinarily rare in business today, and it would have been impossible to do a project like this without it. Neither of us had a choice, but I'll deal with Stan, and happily so, on a handshake any day of the week."

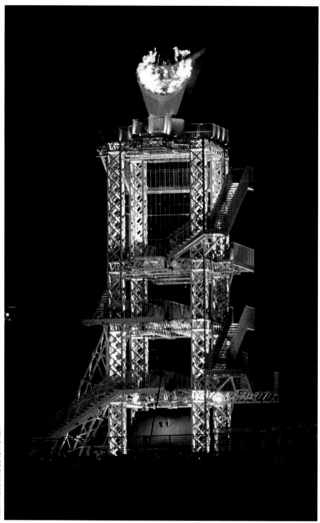

The Olympic cauldron aglow.

BEFORE BASEBALL,
THERE WAS . . .

Before there was Turner Field, there was a parking lot at what is now 755 Hank Aaron Drive. But between the demise of the asphalt slab and the rise of the grand ballpark, there was a little get-together on that same parcel of land in southeast Atlanta that the world will not soon forget. Suffice it to say that the 1996 Centennial Olympic Games left a legacy that will forever challenge the spirit and accomplishments of Braves baseball, no matter what heights it may reach.

Muhammad Ali. Carl Lewis. Michael Johnson. Randy Barnes. Gail Devers. Donovan Bailey. Gwen Torrence and Derrick Adkins. Jackie Joyner-Kersee. Kenny Harrison. Charles Austin. Marie-Jose Perec. Dan O'Brien. Josia Thugwane.

Some are household names. Others didn't register before or after the Olympics on the attention screen of most Americans. But for the 17-day period from July 19-August 4, they all thrilled thousands of spectators and millions of worldwide television viewers with their skill, courage and exploits.

Remarkably, no formal name was ever given to the building that hosted the world's premier track and field athletes and would later, with a little work, become Turner Field. It was called Olympic Stadium, the Olympic stadium, and occasionally, Centennial Olympic Stadium. It seated some 80,000 — 30,000 more than it does today — and was built around a large, burnt-orange oval track destined to be scorched even more by rampaging runners.

The festivities began with the Opening Ceremony. Tickets sold for as much as $636 apiece — before scalping. More than 5,500 people performed in costumes bearing 1.6 million sequins. The parade of nations counted a record 197. Gladys Knight and Celine Dion sang. Thirty chrome pick-up trucks glistened. Nearly 11,000 athletes recited the Olympic oath. The president of the United States declared the Games "open." Evander Holyfield carried the torch into the stadium, and time stood still when Ali — still The Greatest — emerged to light the cauldron.

And that was only the beginning.

What followed was some of the highest drama in Olympic and sports history, all crammed into 10 memorable days of action and reaction. The zeniths reached included:

▌At age 35, Carl Lewis almost didn't qualify for the long jump finals in seeking a fourth straight Olympic gold in his specialty. Approaching his final jump, he ranked 15th and needed to be at least 12th to advance. He responded with the best qualifying leap — 27' 2 1/2" — and the next day jumped 27' 10 3/4" to win his ninth Olympic gold overall.

◼ Johnson, in dominating fashion accentuated by gold shoes, won both the 200 and 400 meters, the first man ever to do so in the Olympics. He set an Olympic record in the 400, then broke his own world record in the 200.

◼ France's Perec barely beat Johnson to the 200/400 double. She won the 400 to become the first person ever to win an Olympic 400 twice, then three days later won the 200 just before Johnson's double.

◼ Donovan Bailey of Canada won the 100 meters in 9.84 to break the world record by .01 of a second. But his "fastest human" performance had to share the spotlight with the antics of defending champion Linford Christie, who was disqualified after two false starts, then refused to leave the track.

◼ The race of the Games was the women's 100 meters that resulted in a photo finish. Gail Devers of the U.S. became only the second woman ever to win the event in consecutive Olympics. Her time of 10.94 was the same time as that of Jamaica's Marlene Ottey, whose protest of the photo interpretation was denied. Torrence, of nearby Decatur, was third by just .02 of a second.

◼ Torrence satisfied her local fans by winning a gold as the anchor on the U.S. 4x100 relay. And Adkins, a product of Georgia Tech, won the 400-meter hurdles.

◼ Barnes, who was banned from his sport from 1990-92 for testing positive for steroids, won the shot put

Dan O'Brien, decathlon champion.

in extraordinary style, going from sixth place to first on his last heave.

◼ Harrison won the gold in the triple jump, twice breaking the U.S. and Olympic records and beating world record holder Jonathan Edwards of Great Britain.

◼ Austin of the U.S. came from second place to win the high jump with an Olympic record of 7' 10". He did so with only one chance at the height after passing at 7' 9 1/4".

◼ At age 34, Joyner-Kersee had to withdraw in tears from the heptathlon due to a hamstring injury, but six days later, with her right leg heavily taped, she won the bronze in the long jump. It was her sixth Olympic medal, the most ever by an American woman in track and field.

ALLEN EYESTONE

Muhammad Ali, always the greatest.

▌ O'Brien overcame his embarrassing failure to qualify for the '92 Games to win the decathlon with an Olympic record of 8,824 points.

▌ Thugwane won the closest men's marathon in Olympic history to become the first black from South Africa to earn Olympic gold.

When the flame had been doused and the Paralympics were completed, they cut up the orange track and sold it for $19.95 a square. The Olympic stadium was reshaped into Turner Field, and Braves baseball assumed center stage. But memories of the 1996 Centennial Olympic Games will always linger fondly on the grounds at 755 Hank Aaron Drive.

COUNTDOWN TO OPENING DAY

Following the 17 days of the Olympics, the Paralympics were staged at the stadium, cutting three weeks that weren't originally planned from the retrofit schedule. On August 26, 1996, however, cranes and workers finally began their assault on dismantling the seating bowl at the north end. Their ultimate goal: Turn an oval into a diamond in time for the opening of the 1997 baseball season. They didn't know it at the time, but they would have just 215 days until the Braves hosted the New York Yankees for a March 29 exhibition game.

The heat was on.

"We did $50 million worth of work in seven months," said Chuck Winstead, group president of Beers Construction that headed a team of contractors that included H.J. Russell & Company and C.D. Moody Construction Company. "That's such a short time frame to tear down half of a stadium, tear out the inside that was used for the Olympics, and then build it all back.

"So many people — a lot of them experts in the industry — said it couldn't be done. Even a month and a half before the opening, people were saying it couldn't be done. If enough people tell you that, you start to think maybe they're right. One of the biggest challenges was keeping in the minds of the troops that we could do it. Once you can convince people they can do something, they usually do it. And the spirit on this job was phenomenal. They decided they were going to do it and show everybody they were wrong . . . and they did."

Winstead said that as many as 770 workers were on the job at the peak as they pushed toward the opening. Not only that, but many were working longer shifts, often even double shifts, toward the end.

Among the major tasks required was hauling in and dumping over 6,000 truckloads of dirt at the north end so that the entry plaza would be level with Ralph David Abernathy Boulevard.

Perhaps the biggest obstacle that had to be overcome was something no one could control — rain. In order to put in the base for the high-tech turf system that was being used, the sub-base terrain had to be completely dry. But near-constant February rain threatened to make that impossible.

At one point, a helicopter was brought in to try to dry the field, a tactic that proved worthless. On two occasions, all the mud was scraped away, only to have more rain create more mud.

"If it had rained one more day, we wouldn't have made it," said Helfrich.

To some extent, that was true. They wouldn't have been able to put in the turf system they wanted, but there were contingencies for a less-complicated installation to get through the first season.

"The day I knew for sure we were going to make it was when we scheduled 48 hours solid for hauling sand in from Macon and we used every truck we could find," Winstead said.

That was in mid-February, and the final tally was 8,200 tons of sand. Once that was down, they were able to follow with the plastic barrier that was required for the sod system.

Aside from removing the Olympic track and replacing it with a pristine baseball field and aside from the massive displacement of concrete and steel that was required to reshape the building, there were plenty of other tasks to be dealt with.

The Braves, mainly Kasten and Smith, had decided there's only one true "opening," and they wanted this one to be "grand." Just having the ballpark far enough along to play a game wasn't satisfactory. They wanted to get every possible aspect of it completed — including such signature amenities as the innovative Scout's Alley, the Ivan Allen Jr. Braves Museum and Hall of Fame, and the Chop House

Atlanta-Fulton County Stadium watches its replacement take shape.

restaurant. The team's offices would have to wait, as would the exclusive 755 Club and a late addition — Coca-Cola Sky Field. But for the most part, the public was going to get a full taste of what, along the way, had officially been named Turner Field.

Coart Johnson, construction manager for Turner Properties, was in charge of making sure it all came together on time and within budget.

"It was the most intense experience I've ever had," Johnson said of the seven-month retrofit. "I saw the schedule and I knew we had a chance. And I couldn't very well go to Stan and say we're not going to make it. Thirty to 40 days out, meetings were called (to discuss the possibility of not being ready to open), but I wouldn't have any part of them.

"I had to tell the Recreation Authority by March 1

Located just south of the old stadium, Turner Field is flanked on the west by Interstates 75 and 85.

if we couldn't do it so they could get the old stadium cleaned up. The second week of February, if it had rained any more, I could have told them, because you can't play baseball without a field. Stan was in my office every day asking if we were going to make it. But by the third week of February, we were very happy. The momentum really picked up around March 1. It was a thrilling project to work on."

Among other things, Johnson had to make last-minute modifications to get an authentic railroad car into the museum as the centerpiece of a major exhibit; he had to jump through hoops to get the city to approve major exterior visuals, such as the Big Ball in the plaza and the larger Turner Field sign over Monument Grove; and he had to figure out how to mount 90-foot high foul poles without putting a crane on the field.

"We couldn't get on the field when we were ready to put in the foul poles," Johnson said. "So we laid them out in the old south parking lot across the street and a helicopter came in, picked them up, carried them over, and set them in flagpole foundations. It was pretty exciting. The train I wasn't too pleased about, but we got it in. The Big Ball was a heckuva problem. It was all ready to go up, but we couldn't go ahead with it until we got a variance on the city sign ordinance at the last second."

So it was that on March 29, 1997, Turner Field was opened for an exhibition game against the defending World Series champion New York Yankees. That and the following afternoon's game served as dress rehearsals for the official First Game that came April 4 against the Cubs. The grass was green, the paint was dry, the bright yellow foul poles stood at attention, the Big Ball hovered over the bustling plaza, and hundreds of fans even walked through the train car in the museum, never sensing the agony it took to roll it into place.

"Turner Field is a compendium of what's great about other parks and franchises," said Smith in describing the final creation.

"Whenever you do something like this for the public, you don't know how it will all work until you've got 50,000 people in it. Then, it's an unbelievable feeling, but it's not yours anymore.

"When you first see all these people without credentials and hard hats, you feel they're violating your space. But that's why you do it, so people will embrace it and enjoy it. That's the way it should be. The big moment is when you realize there's nothing bizarre or wrong about the playing field, after the last out of the first game."

What does it all mean for the fans? There's the obvious: Turner Field is a great place to watch a ballgame and just as great of a place to have an enjoyable — even exciting — outing in a wholesome atmosphere while soaking up all the many aspects of Braves baseball that have combined to make the team the most popular in the majors.

Then there's the perhaps not-so-obvious.

"Teams that are stuck in old stadiums are not competitive and don't have $55 million payrolls," said Kasten. "Without this, we probably would have been in the suburbs. Certainly, if not for the Olympics, we wouldn't have as grand a facility.

"Larry Lucchino, who developed Camden Yards, said two things after touring Turner Field: It has tremendous revenue potential and it is SO pretty. The whole place has come together and is looking so pretty. And I am very proud."

Some 8,200 tons of sand were used in the building of the base for the turf.

MAX ANTON BIRNKAMMER

Turner Field is named for Ted Turner, but it's also a monument to Hank Aaron and his achievements.

TED & HANK

A NAME THAT'S QUITE APROPOS

Where would the Braves be today and in what condition would we find them if Ted Turner had not bought the franchise in 1976? Would the Braves have developed into the Team of the '90s? Would the team be playing in a sparkling new ballpark? Would the franchise still be in Atlanta?

Though these questions are impossible to answer, it is a virtual certainty that the state of Braves baseball wouldn't be as bright as it is today if not for the man in whose honor Turner Field is named.

Oh, perhaps he stuck his finger in the pie a little too much in the early years. We'll forgive him for considering renaming the team the Eagles and for threatening to move some home games to New Orleans and Washington, D.C. After all, he didn't do either.

And yes, his managerial record (0-1, .000) couldn't be any worse.

But at least he meant well back when he was signing free agents such as Andy Messersmith, Gary Matthews and Al "The Mad Hungarian" Hrabosky and when he was getting himself suspended by commissioner Bowie Kuhn. He was a maverick, perhaps even an outlaw by the standards of the baseball establishment. But he always wanted to win, and even though it took him a while to figure out how to

make that happen, he turned the Braves into the most popular baseball team in America with the TBS Superstation and thrust the franchise into its most prosperous period of the 20th century.

Turner Field? It's really quite apropos.

In 1977, Turner became manager for a day.

 ATLANTA BRAVES

FOUNTAINE LEWIS

Turner shows off his 1996 NL Championship ring as Time Warner chairman Gerald Levin inspects his new jewelry.

"It wasn't something that I was going to do," said Turner of his name hanging on the new Home of the Braves. "It had to be forced on me, but I do feel honored. Gerry Levin (chairman of Turner Broadcasting System parent Time Warner Inc.) said we were going to do it when the company was bought. And he's the boss. So I couldn't very well take issue with him. He didn't ask my permission. He made the announcement that he was going to do it."

In fact, Levin surprised even the Braves when he told the world on September 26, 1996, that the ballpark would be named after Turner. The official name "Turner Field" wasn't even announced until nearly three months later, December 13.

Now vice-chairman of Time Warner, a position he assumed on October 10, 1996, Turner oversees

the assets of TBS, including the Braves, the Atlanta Hawks of the National Basketball Association, and the Atlanta Thrashers who will begin play in the National Hockey League in 1999. The TBS umbrella also includes Cable News Network (CNN), Turner Network Television (TNT), the Superstation, Headline News, CNN International, CNN/SI, Turner Classic Movies, Cartoon Network, CNN Airport Network, CNNfn and numerous other subsidiaries.

Turner bought the Braves on January 14, 1976, from the Atlanta/LaSalle Corporation, the syndicate of businessmen headed by current Braves chairman Bill Bartholomay that moved the franchise from Milwaukee to Atlanta in 1966. Turner was just 37 at the time, the youngest owner in baseball.

"One of my goals in life was to be surrounded by unpretentious, rich young men," he once said. "Then I bought the Braves and I was surrounded by 25 of them."

He must have wondered what he'd gotten himself into. The Braves finished in last place with a 70-92 record in his first year of ownership, and they stayed at the division bottom each of the ensuing three seasons, as well. With the exception of 1982, when the team won the National League West and the next two years when they placed second, the Braves were dead last in eight of the first 15 years Turner owned the club and failed to win even half their games in 12 of those seasons.

Nevertheless, Turner always gave Braves fans a show — one way or another.

He immediately served notice of his presence in 1976 by signing Messersmith, an accomplished starting pitcher who'd become the game's first modern free agent by playing out his contract with the Dodgers. Turner gave Messersmith a three-year contract for $1 million and quickly issued him jersey No. 17 with the "nickname" Channel above it to promote his small UHF television station. The lords of baseball were outraged. They ordered Turner to take Messersmith's "nickname" off his jersey, but there was nothing they could do about the advent of free agency. It was a change that was inevitable, yet one that Turner played a major role in implementing.

In 1977, Turner was fined $10,000 and suspended by Kuhn for a year for "tampering" in the signing of Matthews, a free agent outfielder. With the suspension being contested in the courts, Turner was able to continue as team president. That allowed him to pull one of his most famous stunts. On May 11, Turner sent Braves manager Dave Bristol on a 10-day leave that he referred to as a "scouting trip" and then took over in the dugout as manager. The Braves lost, 2-1, at Pittsburgh — their 17th straight defeat — and National League president Chub Feeney promptly ordered Turner out of the dugout.

When Kuhn's suspension of Turner was upheld, the Braves owner simply went off that summer to conduct a successful defense of the America's Cup as captain of the *Courageous*. In the process, he earned the nickname Captain Outrageous.

The Braves were so horrible in the early years of Turner's ownership that they had trouble drawing fans. They tried all sorts of offbeat promotions to increase attendance, and Turner often took part himself in such exploits as bathtub racing, ostrich races, and even pushing a baseball around the bases with his nose.

However, as the demands of growing TBS began to mushroom, Turner was forced to spend less and less time with the Braves. He put Stan Kasten in charge as president and brought Bobby Cox back from Toronto to be general manager. In doing so, he also gave them the freedom and the budget that eventually led to the hiring of John Schuerholz, Cox's return to the dugout as manager, the Braves' stunning vault "From Worst to First" in 1991, and

their continued dominance as the most accomplished team of the decade.

"Like any other Braves fan, I've had hours of disappointment and grief when they were losing, and then many more moments of joy and celebration when they were winning," Turner said. "Winning the World Series was one of the biggest . . . at the very top of my wish list."

That, of course, took place in 1995. It was the Braves' first World Championship since 1957 and the first major sports league championship ever for Atlanta.

"I'm sorry we've only won one World Series so far, but we came close to winning more," Turner said. "A timely hit, a timely out, we could have won a couple or three. But at least we were there. At the rate we're going, we'll play every team in the American League in another 10 years. We've played four different ones so far in the Series."

Born on November 19, 1938 in Cincinnati — also the birthplace of professional baseball — Turner attended Brown University. After working in the family advertising business in Savannah for several years, he purchased Channel 17, an independent station, in 1970. On December 17, 1976, he originated the "superstation" concept by transmitting the station's signal to cable systems nationwide via satellite. And the Braves were the centerpiece of his programming.

Over the next two decades, Turner became not only one of the most influential individuals in the television and entertainment industries, but also one of the most recognized people in the world.

On June 1, 1980, he launched CNN, the world's first 24-hour all-news TV network. And on January 1, 1982, Headline News began operation.

In 1991, Turner was selected Man of the Year by *Time* magazine, primarily for the worldwide significance of CNN's coverage of the Persian Gulf War.

Here's the windup . . . and here's the pitch!

He is an active environmentalist and has received numerous civic and industry honors.

While the future of many major league baseball teams and their ability to contend annually for championships seems to be in constant turmoil due to the game's volatile economics, Turner leaves no doubt about his expectations and intentions for the Braves.

"No one ever wins forever, not even the mighty Yankees," he said. "But as long as I'm alive, I hope the team strives for and achieves as much excellence as is humanly possible . . . that we do the best job that we can."

That's the sort of commitment all Braves fans can understand and appreciate. But what else would be expected from a man who's changed the world and become a billionaire in the last 20 years, not to mention overseen the Braves' meteoric ascent to baseball's penthouse?

Remember, the ballpark has his name on it. He's not about to let that good name be embarrassed by its residents. Ted Turner and the Braves have come too far and been through too much for that to happen without putting up quite a fight.

J. STOLL

THE LION'S DEN

For a baseball fan, visiting Turner Field can be a bit like a trip to The Land of Oz. And for the lucky few who arrive as guests of the ballpark's namesake, well, they may really feel like they're "Off to See The Wizard."

Entering Ted Turner's private suite just below his private box is not unlike walking into Dorothy's Kansas storm cellar. In fact, its nickname is "the bunker" because it is a few steps below field level. And to give Turner's guests that true Yellow Brick Road feeling, they are greeted at the field entrance to the suite by a Lion's Den sign, featuring the smiling Cowardly Lion himself. The sign is a memento of the restaurant of the same name that used to be at the CNN Center.

The carpeted suite is used by Turner and his wife, Jane Fonda, to entertain before, during and after games. It's comfortable but not lavish and is tastefully decorated with reminders of the Braves' success in the '90s. Furnishings are limited to a sofa, four chairs, a coffee table and a credenza/bookcase. There's a wet bar, complete with ice machine, a restroom, and naturally, a television and telephone.

Many of the framed photos on the walls feature Turner (with the '95 World Series trophy; getting a championship ring; with his wife; with Bill Lucas, the late Braves executive). But the most unusual is an elongated, fish-eye cover shot of Turner Field taken on Opening Night just as Turner was throwing out the first pitch.

Out in the stands, Turner's box consists of 46 blue seats cordoned off by a green railing and white chain in rows 1-5 of section 107. As all Braves fans know, the box is located just to the left of the home dugout, and though it is a long way from Kansas, it's still tantalizingly close to Oz.

Ted Turner's suite is decorated with reminders of championship seasons.

FIT FOR THE KING

There is only one all-time home run king, and he is —and quite likely always will be — Henry Louis Aaron, the greatest of all Braves. Lest anyone ever forget that, or should someone ever need to learn about it, Turner Field stands proudly and boldly at 755 Hank Aaron Drive, fittingly the grandest monument ever constructed to a ballplayer.

From its address to the name of its swanky private restaurant — the 755 Club — Turner Field is one colossal memorial to Aaron and his accomplishments, including his 755 lifetime home runs.

"He towered above them all because he broke the record," said the man for whom Turner Field is named but who otherwise takes a back seat to his long-time employee at the Braves' new ballpark.

"The record" Ted Turner mentioned, of course,

came April 8, 1974, when Aaron hit his 715th career home run, surpassing Babe Ruth's total. Though that is the most well-known and exalted of the incomparable outfielder's achievements, it almost disguises his overall value as a ballplayer. Aaron may sit atop all power hitters in the record book, but he was no mere slugger. In fact, for most of his career, he was never thought of in such terms because he was so accomplished in all phases of the game.

"The Hammer" or "Hammerin' Hank" as he was known, also could hit for average, hit in the clutch, run, field (three Gold Gloves) and throw, all with a grace and style seldom seen from other ballplayers. And eventually, Aaron's machine-like consistency and durability enabled him to wrest the most glamorous of all records from the most charismatic figure in baseball history.

During his 23-year major league career, Aaron

CHRIS HAMILTON

Hank Aaron and Tom Glavine (l) complete the ceremonial transfer of home plate from Atlanta-Fulton County stadium.

Atlanta mayor Bill Campbell (r) makes Turner Field's new address official.

was named an All-Star in every season except his first and last. He ranks first all-time in runs batted in (2,297) and extra-base hits (6,856) and is second in at-bats and runs, third in games and hits, and ninth in doubles. He holds more offensive records than anyone else ever to play the game and was the first player to compile both 500 home runs and 3,000 hits.

En route to a .305 career batting average, the Mobile, Alabama, native won two National League batting titles (1956 and '59), led the NL in home runs four times, and was voted the league's MVP in 1957 when the Braves won the World Series. He batted .357 in his only League Championship Series ('69) and .364 in two World Series ('57 and '58).

Turner Field is not only the rarest of diamonds, but also a shrine to the rarest of ballplayers.

"I'm very grateful, very thankful that there are so many things here with my name on them," said Aaron, now a senior vice-president of the Braves and Turner Broadcasting and assistant to Braves president Stan Kasten.

Though Aaron's responsibilities are chiefly with Turner's Airport Channel, he moved his office from the CNN Center to Turner Field shortly after the Braves' office staff moved into their new quarters at mid-season.

"I enjoyed being at the CNN Center, but I love being here," Aaron said from his Turner Field office, located just above left field and right under the 755 Club from where he has a choice view of the playing field.

"I feel more at home here. It's where I grew up — on the ballfield."

And where else should Hank Aaron park his briefcase than at 755 Hank Aaron Drive?

On the eve of the first regular-season game at Turner Field, the City of Atlanta renamed a two-mile stretch of Capitol Avenue, which runs north-south along the east side of the new ballpark, in honor of Aaron. It's quite a tribute — but just the first of many.

On Opening Night, much to the delight of the capacity crowd, it was Aaron who emerged from the gate in the center-field wall to complete the transfer of a ceremonial home plate from Atlanta-Fulton County Stadium to Turner Field. The thunderous ovation he received thrilled him to the bone.

"I felt like I was walking on a cloud," he admitted. "It was a tear-jerking moment. There aren't many times when I get tears in my eyes, but I did that night. I was quite thrilled."

The dominant image of Turner Field that fans see as they approach the ballpark from its north side is a 100-foot-high image of a baseball on the back of the scoreboard and hovering over the plaza. It's not just any ball — but the one the Dodgers' Al Downing threw and Aaron propelled into the night on April 8, 1974. It's the same 715 ball visitors can finally see — after it was locked in a vault for years — in the Ivan Allen Jr. Braves Museum at Turner Field. Yes, the magical bat is there, too, along with Aaron's old locker and many other items from his career.

"I'm glad the ball and bat are on display here," Aaron said. "It's theirs. I hit it here in Atlanta. It belongs to the people of Atlanta and the Southeast.

"That museum is really special . . . all the gloves and bats and balls and all the other things to see. I'll tell you, I remember riding on that train, but I don't remember it being that big," he said with a laugh, referring to the sleeper car in the museum that helps bring to life the Braves' Milwaukee era. "When I was a rookie, they put you down there under the wheels. And when the train went through a curve, you could feel it. The next year, I moved up a little, and eventually I got up with the big boys."

Indeed.

Just outside the museum in Monument Grove are the statue and bust of Aaron that used to be on display at Atlanta-Fulton County Stadium, as well as a new memorial to his retired uniform No. 44. Above the entrances to Turner Field, fans see a silhouette of Aaron's 715th home run swing. Likewise, a similar silhouette will adorn the seat standard at the end of each row.

Scout's Alley includes a floor-to-ceiling blowup of the Braves' scouting report on Aaron when he played with the Indianapolis Clowns of the old Negro leagues. A nearby interactive exhibit shows where in the strike zone Aaron most liked to hit pitches. And the new parking lot on the old site of Atlanta-Fulton County Stadium includes a monument to No. 715. A duplication of the old outfield wall, some 28 feet wide, has been erected in tempered glass to replicate the plexiglass used in 1974. Behind it, mounted on a backdrop representing the former outfield grandstand, is the "715" sign from the old stadium.

The man himself appreciates it all, but he also has quite a liking for the big picture of Turner Field.

"I've never seen a ballpark as pretty as this one," he said. "It's very well thought-out. I've been to (Baltimore's) Camden Yards, and I don't think it touches this. When you're talking stadiums, this has got to be the jewel. It's everything you could want. There's something for everyone. When ballparks are designed in the future, they're going to be designed like this one."

However, there will be one huge difference. Only Turner Field has "The Hammer."

On April 8, 1974, a new all-time home run king was crowned.

Appropriately, Hank Aaron now keeps his office at Turner Field.

THE BIG BALL

It rules the front door to Turner Field. It's the Big Ball, No. 715.

As fans approach Turner Field from the north, the Big Ball lets them know well in advance that their journey to the Home of the Braves is almost complete.

In terms of both its significance and its 100' x 100' size, it must surely be the biggest baseball ever captured and enlarged on film.

Deciding what would serve as the "central icon" of the entry plaza to Turner Field was a major obstacle for the Braves and the ballpark's design team.

"There was a lot of debate about the Big Ball in model form, about whether it was enough to carry the plaza," said Janet Marie Smith, now vice-president of sports and entertainment facilities for Turner

Properties. "We put a lot of pressure on ourselves to create a central icon . . . we had fountains, a big baseball floating in the water, a tomahawk . . .

"The day we came up with the idea of the baseball, there were about 15 of us in the room. We decided all the elements we had were so contrived, so we pushed them aside and tried again.

"DAIQ (D'Agostino Izzo Quirk Architects) had a big baseball on a construction document. There was one in the office, and we said, 'What's obvious?' We said, 'What if we took a baseball and essentially it became a movie screen?' It was Ted Ryan (of the Atlanta History Center) who said, 'If it's a baseball, it ought to be Hank Aaron's baseball.'

"Someone asked if it would be enough to animate the plaza, and at the end of the day, we all said, 'Yes.' We gave a big sigh of relief. We'd found the focal point.

"I think it's incredible. If it was just the ball, it would be less compelling, but with the TVs, the video board, the message on the ticker . . ."

And, by the way, has anyone called Guinness?

The 'Big Ball' provides a Turner Field icon that beckons fans from blocks away.

Ryan Klesko shows that pitchers aren't the only Braves who relax on the putting green.

The Home of
the Braves

The GM's perspective

John Schuerholz's mother, 77-year-old Maryne Schuerholz, only gets to Atlanta from her Baltimore home once each baseball season. And like every other Braves fan, the first thing she wanted to see when she arrived in the summer of '97 was Turner Field.

"I'm picking her up at the airport this afternoon, and she said she wants to come here first, not our home or anywhere else," Schuerholz said one August morning in Turner Field's inaugural season.

A week later, he reported, "So, I brought her right here and gave her a golf-cart tour. She saw everything — the plaza, Scout's Alley, Tooner Field, the 755 Club. She said, 'It looks so gorgeous on TV, but it's even more beautiful in person.' She watches every night on TV, and she thought it's a lot bigger in person than it looks on TV. She thought it was really fascinating to see all the things kids can do."

Like everyone else in the Braves' front office, Schuerholz is proud of the Braves' new home, and he enjoys showing it to people — especially his mother.

"It was really exciting for me to do that," said the architect of the Braves' success. "It was wonderful because this place turned out so great. It's like when you're building a new home and you don't know how it will turn out. Then all of a sudden it's gorgeous, and you want to share it with everyone. That's the way we feel about this place."

The Braves welcomed over 3.4 million fans to Turner Field in 1997, but few, if any, got a glimpse of the personal suite Schuerholz and Braves president Stan Kasten share on the press box level behind home plate.

"It's just to the left of the 'H' in Home of the Braves," Schuerholz said, locating the suite in reference to the large sign on the club level behind home plate.

Neither plush nor spacious, the suite is certainly comfortable but probably more practical than many fans would expect. It's professionally appointed, more an extension of Schuerholz and Kasten's offices than anything else. There's not even a private restroom.

The most distinctive feature are two televisions built right into the counter top at the front window of the suite where the two executives sit. The TV screens are flush with the counter top, allowing them, so to speak, to keep one eye on the action on the field and the other eye on whatever game or games they're tracking on TV. Just like the bank of TVs in the plaza, those in this suite — thanks to a satellite dish — can be tuned to any major league game that's being televised at any given moment.

The only decoration on the walls is a photograph of the four championship rings the Braves have won in the '90s.

"That's our mission statement," said Schuerholz. Swinging open the two windows (one of which bears

Braves president Stan Kasten (l) and general manager John Schuerholz share a private box that's an extension of their offices.

a distinct white scar from a foul ball) at the front of the box provides a dynamic panorama of Turner Field, as well as a "feel" for seemingly the entire ballpark.

Though Schuerholz said the suite "seats 8-10 comfortably," he admitted he's "a very bad host." But who can blame him? Watching Braves games is his job, not his pastime.

Just as the game is ready to start, he pulls out his "tools" — binoculars, the Braves media guide, and the latest statistics and notes on the two teams. Naturally, a telephone (black, not red) is within easy reach on the counter.

"This is everything I need to watch a ballgame," Schuerholz said, "this and those guys down there."

THE FIELD GENERAL'S HEADQUARTERS

It's a mid-season's Sunday morning, and Bobby Cox is stretched out on a comfortable blue sofa, watching his ceiling-mounted TV and enjoying a cigar in his well-appointed office on the ground level at Turner Field. The previous night's victory is still fresh in his memory and the next battle is only three hours away. Yet a reasonably secure first-place lead allows for a few minutes of relaxation.

Not that Cox's old office at Atlanta-Fulton County Stadium was inadequate for the needs of a big league baseball manager, but his new pad is much more reflective of the stature he's grown into as one of the game's most successful field leaders.

"Turner Field is great," he says. "It's got all the amenities you'd like for the family. They've tried to accommodate the family, and that's important if we're going to build the fan base. If you get the kids in, they'll be fans forever.

"The Chop House is a big hit . . . Scout's Alley . . . all the games for kids. It's very accommodating. It's a very beautiful park."

And Cox's office is one of the more interesting and intriguing niches of the grand baseball palace. It is a monument to the Braves' accomplishments of the '90s and also offers insight to the makeup of this man who has played such a major role in elevating Braves baseball from joke material to a stature that borders on religion for multitudes of fans in the South and throughout the nation.

A smart, mahogany desk and credenza give the impression that this could be the office of a corporate CEO. And the leather briefcase is fitting for such an executive, too. But that's the extent of the pretense here. The rest of the spacious room is filled with memories of a man devoted to baseball and the outdoors.

The trophies include:

▮ A handsome pair of largemouth bass mounted on one wall: "I caught them both on the same day after a spring training game in Lakeland a few year ago. The one on the left is close to 10 pounds and the other is 8 1/2 or 9."

▮ A nearly floor-to-ceiling, black, feather-like fin from an Alaskan baleen whale: "(Childhood friend and former Braves pitcher) Wade Blasingame gave me that. It's a heckuva conversation piece."

▮ Two stuffed quail sitting near his well-stocked cigar chest: "Ted (Turner) takes John (Schuerholz) and me to his plantation every year. He was nice enough to have those mounted and sent to me from New Mexico."

▮ Above the quail is a picture of Cox, Turner and Schuerholz, shotguns shouldered, during another hunting excursion to Florida.

▮ Dominating the opposite wall is a large, plaque-like memento of the Braves' 34 years of spring training in West Palm Beach. It consists of two crossed bats, a ball, a first baseman's mitt, a catcher's mask and the team logo: "That's from Manero's. It hung over the Braves' table for years, and (restaurant owner) John Mahoney gave it to me as a going-away gift."

Bobby Cox's office offers insight to the manager and the man.

The players have a special parking lot directly adjacent to the south side of the ballpark.

▌On top of the credenza are two cowboy hats, one new and one worn, made by a friend of Cox's, Gus Miller of Cincinnati: "The one on this side I wore to the park every day in '91. It worked pretty good, so I keep it around for luck."

▌Opposite Cox's desk, on a set of base cabinets, are three autographed baseballs in a case. The signatures are those of Tom Glavine, Greg Maddux and John Smoltz: "It's not often you have three Cy Young winners on the same team."

Commemorative bats, balls and awards from various All-Star Games and World Series appearances, once rare finds, are scattered about like common knickknacks, treasured for sure, yet increasingly common in this man's office.

The credenza also holds plenty of family pictures,

an honorary badge Cox was given by Olympics security officers, and two unopened bottles of champagne, a reminder of many joyous celebrations across the street.

Behind the credenza, a wall cordons off Cox's private dressing area and shower.

"This office is where I spend most of my time, here and back in the training room talking to (trainer) Dave (Pursley)," says Cox. "We have our (staff) meetings for each series in the conference room next door. That's worked out great. And the putting green down the hall is a great place to kill time, especially during rain delays.

"The dugout is a lot better here. The old one was more like a bunker, it was too deep. I think this is the best dugout in baseball, for me. There's plenty of room. We can't see in the bullpens, but we have TV monitors that show both bullpens. Each manager has that, so it's no problem.

"It's just all very well thought out. (Braves presi-

The circular layout of lockers gives the players space yet allows them to communicate.

dent) Stan (Kasten) was at the forefront. I know he's very proud, and he should be. It took a lot of time and effort to make it all work — and it does."

With that, Cox was off to attend to one of the countless details that lead to winning another game — and hopefully another championship . . . details he could handle in any office, any clubhouse, any ballpark, but details that are so much more enjoyable and so much less taxing in the uptown environment down under Turner Field.

THE INNER SANCTUM

On a typical game day, Tom Glavine drives to Turner Field from his home in the suburbs north of Atlanta during the mid-afternoon. He exits the interstate system and quickly finds himself heading south on Hank Aaron Drive. He passes the remainder of Atlanta-Fulton County Stadium, where he pitched a game for the ages — eight innings of one-hit ball in decisive Game 6 of the 1995 World Series. Continuing past Turner Field, he takes a sharp right at Love Street on the southeast corner of the new ballpark, then takes another quick right into the gated players' parking area directly adjacent to his new home away from home.

In a matter of seconds, Glavine is inside the ballpark, making a quick walk through the ground-level corridor and into the Braves' posh clubhouse. He stops by the cushy players' lounge to get a cup of coffee and heads for his locker, located strategically at the top of the circle in the keyhole-shaped room (a circle on top of a rectangle).

It's actually the back of the clubhouse, a location Glavine chose because it's close to the weight room

Tom Glavine says "no detail was overlooked" at Turner Field.

and trainer's room, where he spends a lot of time, and it also affords him the best view of the other 43 lockers, his teammates and their activities, the coaching staff, and the media and other visitors. It's the ideal spot for the team's elder statesman in terms of continuous service.

"I was probably the first to pick a spot," Glavine said. "I was here a couple of times in the winter, and I told (assistant equipment manager) Casey (Stevenson) in Florida what I wanted. I imagine the veteran guys had first dibs. I like it because I can go back there (trainer's/weight rooms) and watch TV, but the biggest factor is I can see everything."

All the lockers are identical. They're spacious, made of oak, and have several compartments. At floor level, there's a nook with a combination lock for valuables, but Glavine said he only stows toiletries there, preferring to use a community lock box for his wallet, watch, etc. He also keeps several pairs of shoes in the lower level. Above the bar for hanging uniforms and street clothes, are two more cabinets. He keeps gloves in the lower of the two and his equipment bag and extra shoes in the top level.

"I'm probably a neat freak compared to some of the other guys," Glavine said of his orderly space. "I like to be able to find things."

The lefthander said he moved all the trinkets, like his Bart Simpson doll, from his old locker at Atlanta-Fulton County but wound up throwing out most of

54

what he had collected since being promoted to Atlanta August 14, 1987.

"Bart is gone," he said. "I figured: A new stadium, I should start over and clear out some stuff."

His personal possessions consist mainly of pictures of his daughter, Amber, a framed four-leaf clover someone sent him, assorted caps, a picture of the Blue Angels precision flight team, and a couple of hockey sticks.

In front of each locker is a red director's chair with the Braves logo on the inside of the back and Coca-Cola on the outside. Much of the floor space in the center of the carpeted clubhouse is taken by two large picnic tables and two round tables. The players eat, chat, read and sign balls at the picnic tables and play cards at the round tables. Baskets for dirty clothes and trash cans are located throughout the room.

"The clubhouse is really comfortable," Glavine said. "I think there were two concerns: You didn't want it to be too big, because the guys would be so spread out that you lose the unity and team feeling. And you didn't want it to be too small for the obvious reasons.

"I think this is just right, and there's still room for when they expand the roster in September.

"It's comfortable, but everyone feels like they belong. A lot has to do with the shape. In the old one, Blauser and Lemke were always around that corner and you couldn't see them. It was almost like they weren't around. You lose a little unity that way. Here, everyone is visible."

The decor is strictly "championship." There's a large gold sign commemorating the Braves' '95 World Series victory and four white signs emblematic of the National League pennants won in the '90s.

As has been the case in the Braves' clubhouse for nearly a decade, there's no music blaring. Chuck Tanner, who left in 1988, was the last manager to allow music, Glavine pointed out.

"It's hard to have music because there are so many different tastes," Glavine said. "The best way to control it is to not have any at all. That's the way it's been since the late '80s."

Television is another matter. There are four built-in TVs just below the ceiling at the center of the room. Two face forward and two backward. There are two more built into the walls, one on the left and one on the right. Several baseball games and other sports events often play simultaneously, but the volume is muffled or muted.

"There are enough TVs to show enough choices for everyone," Glavine said. "The only time it might be a problem is on the weekend if there are a lot of different football or basketball games on."

Even then, a player doesn't have to go very far to find another screen. There are several more, including a wide screen, in the lounge and a few more in the weight room, where the treadmills actually have built-in TVs.

Off the hallway leading to the trainer's room and exercise area are offices for Bill Acree, the equipment manager and director of team travel, and his assistant, Stevenson. Across from them is the bat room that contains nothing but 300 to 400 bats, Acree estimated.

Around the corner is Bobby Cox's office and a conference room used for coaches' meetings and the players' chapel service.

Across from them is a high-tech video room with numerous monitors, VCRs and control panels, along with a laptop computer. It could be a scaled-down network control room, but it has nothing to do with TBS bringing the Braves into your home every evening. It has everything to do with providing the players with the most state-of-the-art facility available to analyze, dissect and review their performance and that of their opponents.

"It's just for the players," Glavine said. "All you have to do is punch into the laptop what you're looking for — your last at-bat, your at-bats against a certain pitcher, how you pitched to a certain batter the last time — and it comes right up on the screen. It's really unbelievable. I don't think anyone else, except maybe the Indians, has anything like this."

On down the hall are the trainer's room (lots of space, lots of tables, whirlpools, etc.) and the weight room (brand-new, baseball-specific machines with Braves logos on the padding).

"No detail was overlooked," Glavine emphasized. Included among the array of features in the 20,000-square-foot facility:

■ The special SwimEx rehabilitation pool he uses to loosen up after starts by swimming against resistance.

■ A sauna.

■ A swing area behind the dugout where pinch-hitters get loose.

■ The two roomy batting cages with pitching mounds that, among other things, allow Braves pitchers to stay loose during rain delays.

■ An X-ray room for quick diagnosis of injuries.

■ Yet another video room, this one right behind the dugout, that is a smaller version of the other one and enables players to quickly review their performance while a game is in progress.

■ And, of course, the much ballyhooed putting green.

The contoured, artificial turf putting green has four holes and is surrounded on two sides by a realistic mural of the 16th hole at Augusta National where the famed Masters is played each April. Braves president Stan Kasten promised the players this amenity if they won the '95 Series.

"It's great. It gives the players a way to relax," Glavine said. "I've even seen the players who don't golf back here. Some people might say it's a distraction, but it can be a positive, because when players get together, they usually wind up talking baseball. And that's how you learn."

Finally, after weaving through all of this, you come to the Braves' dugout. Long and wide, it's much roomier than its predecessor. But just when you think everything's perfect, Glavine offered that it hasn't necessarily always been this way.

"The bench was pine — you talk about catching some splinters," Glavine said with a chuckle. "It's just one of those things they had to find out about. When Denny (Neagle) was coming off the field after the first inning of the first game, we tried to warn him to put a towel down first, but it was too late. You should have seen the splinters all over the seat of his pants. They changed the wood to oak."

Regardless, it's obvious that players' accommodations have come quite a way since the days when all they had was a nail on the wall.

BEYOND THE OUTFIELD WALL

The origin of the word "bullpen" has never been verified by historians. Theories include the presence in the early 20th century of Bull Durham tobacco signs on many outfield fences near where pitchers warmed up, as well as the practice of managers assigning "extra" pitchers to sit in a "penned" off area of the outfield, similar to a place for keeping livestock — including bulls.

Whatever the case, the bullpen has evolved into a locale of great mystique, a private domain for relief pitchers that's generally out of sight and out of mind during most of the game. However, much of that has changed at Turner Field, where the bullpen is in the midst of the party.

The Braves' bullpen is located behind the outfield wall in right-center field, and the visiting team's 'pen has a similar address in left field. In both cases, fans can stand directly over the relievers, separated only by a 15-foot-high overhang.

In the Braves' bullpen, the overhang stops almost directly over the three pitchers' rubbers, providing fans an exciting bird's-eye view of high-speed closer Mark Wohlers and his associates when they're warming up. In fact, the fans occasionally get so distracted that their beverages get away from them.

"They (fans) spill beer on us all the time," said Wohlers. "I've come in (to the game) a couple of times and they say, 'What are you guys doing down there?' I say, 'Sitting by the keg.' The fans are right over us."

Like everything else at Turner Field, the two-tiered bullpen is "state-of-the-art." But there is one

Fans can get a Paul Byrd's (45) eye view of the bullpen.

conspicuous exception. At outfield level, just inside the big gate that swings open to allow relievers access to the field, is an upholstered metal office chair that looks like it saw combat duty in World War II — and barely survived. Dirty and rusty and sporting numerous wounds that ooze upholstery stuffing, it is bandaged extensively with duct tape. On the back, hand-written with a Sharpie, is: Ned's Bullpen Chair.

For all anyone knows, the chair's history could date to the Braves' arrival in Atlanta in 1966. Maybe it even came with them from Milwaukee?

"All I know is that it's been my chair for seven years," said Yost, the Braves' bullpen coach. "It's real comfortable, and when we moved over here, I told (field director) Ed Mangan to be sure to bring it along."

Comfort notwithstanding, the chair's survival at Turner Field undoubtedly stems from that old baseball constant — superstition. Yost arrived as a member of Bobby Cox's staff in 1991. If that chair was good enough to go from "worst to first," it ought to be good enough to stay in first — at any ballpark. Thus far, it's worked well, too.

The first level of the Braves' bullpen consists primarily of two large benches, hidden by the outfield wall. There is, of course, a telephone near Yost's chair that allows him to communicate with the Braves' dugout. It is one of three phones in the 'pen. The other two are on the upper level, one near the three home plates and the other near the pitchers' rubbers.

The warm-up level is eight steps above field level and features an oversized bench that makes the relievers appear small when they sit on it, but gives them an unobstructed view of the game. The warm-up area is completely sodded. There's also a water fountain and a small clock, the latter enabling starting pitchers to pace their pre-game throwing and others to time workouts between appearances.

"The bullpen took some getting used to," admitted Tom Glavine. "People are hollering at you all the time. They want you to look up at them, sign autographs, pose for pictures."

"And they make noises at us . . . 'Whoop . . . whoop!'" said Wohlers.

But, in general, the Braves seem to like the atmosphere and the interaction with fans.

"I love the bullpen," said Denny Neagle. "When you finish warming up and walk out through the gate, the fans start cheering real loud for you. They really get into it. It gives you a boost.

"The other thing I like is you can hear the ball echo off the walls when it hits the catcher's mitt — like at Dodger Stadium. It sounds like everyone's throwing like Wohlers. It's good for your mind. You hear that mitt pop, and you think, 'I must be throwing better than I thought.'"

Unlike Glavine and Neagle, who are starters, reliever Mike Bielecki spends most of his time in the bullpen.

"It's fan-friendly," he said. "The fans get to watch Wohlers throw 100 mph from a perspective where they're only 15 to 20 feet away compared to 100 feet or more in a game. They 'ooh and aah.'

"You get a catcall occasionally. But it's kind of neat. People are trying to get autographs. They'll drop balls, other things down there. And they say it's always their first game or their birthday. They yell at us, and sometimes we'll yell back if we're not warming up. They'll offer to get you a hot dog, but of course, they want to trade the hot dog for a ball."

Sometimes, no barter is needed. Like the day near mid-season when John Smoltz just went over to the ball bag and started grabbing balls, signing them, and tossing them skyward. At Turner Field, sometimes the bullpen can be a ball-pen.

J. STOLL

Ned Yost's war-torn bullpen chair survived the move from Atlanta-Fulton County Stadium.

The Ty Cobb statue is a memorial to a "Georgia Peach" who never played for the Braves.

AROUND THE PARK

THE GREEN, GREEN GRASS OF HOME

Anyone who saw Turner Field a month before its first game would've had a hard time believing the Braves could open on time with a gorgeous, green field under their feet. But they did and there was, proving that Bobby Cox knows his landscaper as well as he knows his ballplayers.

"Ed Mangan is the world's greatest groundskeeper," Cox said of the Braves' field director. "He's such a perfectionist. He can do anything. He could work for NASA building rockets if he wanted to."

We take you now to Mission Control.

There's a knock on the door of the inconspicuous office under the right-field seats at Turner Field. In a moment, a man answers. From his shoes to his Braves cap, he's covered in sand, dirt, water and sweat.

"We had some rain," he says sheepishly. "I've been under the tarp."

This is a rocket scientist?

Well, something like that.

After making himself more presentable, Mangan proceeded to demonstrate what it takes to keep the immaculate playing surface of this new ballpark in top condition.

His office does indeed resemble Mission Control. With the click of the mouse on his desktop computer, Mangan can call up the current satellite radar weather picture, enabling him to monitor any rain in the vicinity of Turner Field. On another computer in an adjacent room, he's testing another radar program.

Also from his desktop computer, he can monitor the water level holding in the elaborate drainage system under the field by reading gauges at four locations. If the level fluctuates more than he'd like, two pumps are automatically activated to add or reduce water.

Ed Mangan workd on making Turner Field come to life.

61

TOMMY BUTLER

Workers beat the odds and the skeptics by sodding the field in time for the opener.

Then with yet another software program — one he designed himself — he can control the 11 zones of the irrigation system.

But even with all the modern gadgetry, having the field ready for its dress rehearsal, the March 29 exhibition game against the Yankees, was never a sure thing.

Starting with what essentially was a mud hole in January, Mangan had about two and a half months to: install a maze of drains and five miles of drain line; grade the surface by laser to insure absolute perfection; cover the field with 135,000 square feet of watertight plastic to create a giant flower pot; cover the plastic with 8,200 tons of sand and three tons of organic fertilizer; laser grade again; lay 120,000 square feet of hybrid (GN-1) Bermuda sod; and get it ready to withstand a full season of Braves baseball.

"The danger was there (that the field wouldn't be ready), but as far as I was concerned, we were going to play — by hook or by crook," said Mangan. "We were going to do whatever necessary to play on the 29th.

We walked a fine line for a while, but I never considered not being ready. I just stayed focused on finding a way to get it ready. We worked from 20 to 23 hours a day, seven days a week to get ready for the opener."

In the process, he and his crew created a thing of beauty.

The sod, some five acres, actually was purchased by the Braves a year in advance and was raised on a turf farm owned by professional golf star Greg "The Shark" Norman in Avon Park, Florida.

The Prescription Athletic Turf system, including the gravity/vacuum drainage system, was designed and engineered by The Motz Group of Cincinnati. Because of the plastic barrier, Mangan said, "The field is 100 percent pure. No water gets in or out unless we say so."

The drainage system incorporates a large drain behind the infield to accommodate rain water dumped off the tarp and vacuum pumps that can suck water off the field at up to three times the pull of gravity. As much as 102,000 gallons of water can be drained per hour, a solution for the heavy late-afternoon and early evening thunderstorms common to Atlanta summers.

"Rainout" is a four-letter word to Mangan, who is in his seventh season with the Braves. With the technology at his disposal and the long hours of work he and his staff put into the preparation and maintenance of the field, he sees no reason for postponement other than heavy rain that just won't go away. Even then, expect him to put up a fight.

"That's why we're here — to play a baseball game," he said. "Through technology, hard work and good men, we'll give the fans what they paid for, what they came to see. It's not acceptable to call a game. We're just not going to let it happen."

Mangan has only one full-time employee and utilizes 15 to 16 part-timers during the season, most of them just working the games. Perhaps their biggest test is getting the 29,000-square-foot tarp on and off when rain comes and goes during a game. Mangan said the tarp weighs one ton — without water — and up to 70,000 to 80,000 pounds with water.

Technology is still no substitute for hard work.

"You have to learn to improvise and do a little of everything in this job," said Mangan, who also maintains a 5,000-square-foot turf farm behind the center-field wall. "If anything goes wrong, you have to fix it. You have to be self-sufficient . . . whatever it takes, even mixing up a little witch's brew."

Witch's brew?

Well, remember, NASA used duct tape to help salvage Apollo 13.

ECHOES OF GREATNESS

There's Warren Spahn, with his classic high leg kick, picking apart National League hitters in the '50s.

There's Eddie Mathews, a ballplayer's ballplayer, smashing home runs at such a pace in the late '50s that some people thought he might catch Babe Ruth. And Hank Aaron, the personification of style and consistency, doing exactly what some thought Mathews would do — but none thought he'd do.

You can almost sense their presence . . . and you can feel their splendor . . . as you stroll through Monument Grove, where the Braves' colorful past meets their glorious present at the north end of Turner Field.

There's Phil Niekro, the workhorse, mystifying batters with his baffling knuckleball and racking up victories with the overmatched Braves of the '70s. And Dale Murphy, the white knight of the '80s, winning back-to-back MVP Awards.

Since the Braves were founded in 1871 as the Boston Red Stockings and joined the National League in its inaugural season of 1876, many of the most-revered players in history have played for the franchise. The memorials in Monument Grove echo the greatness of some of those players, enabling fans to "remember when" while they picnic and take advantage of the excellent photo opportunities afforded by this moving tribute to Braves history. And fans don't even need their tickets to enter this area of the ballpark.

The tree-lined grove also includes a colorful reminder of the team's success through the years. On the back of the west pavilion are pennants showing the years the team has won modern National League (1914, '48, '57, '58, '91, '92, 95, '96) and World Series championships ('14, '57, '95), displayed around giant photos of some of the club's legendary players. Of course, there's space left for future championships, too!

One major addition planned for display in Monument Grove in 1998 is the "hall of fame" portion of the Ivan Allen Jr. Braves Museum and Hall of Fame, where fans will be able to mingle with even more memories from the team's rich past.

WHO ARE THEY?

■ 21 WARREN SPAHN

The winningest lefthander in baseball history, Warren Spahn won 363 career games, a total that trails only Cy Young, Walter Johnson, Christy Mathewson and Grover Cleveland Alexander. Remarkably, Spahn didn't win his first game until age 25 due to three years of military service during World War II. He went on to register a National League record 13 seasons of 20 or more victories. He won all but seven of his games as a Brave from 1946-64, including two no-hitters — the first in 1960 at age 39 and the second the following year, five days after his 40th birthday. In 1963, at age 42, he was 23-7 with seven shutouts, a 2.60 ERA, and led the league in complete games for the seventh straight year — a major league record. Spahn's records are too numerous to detail, but among them are an NL-record (for pitchers) 35 career home runs and a major league record (for pitchers) 82 double plays started. He also was the Major League Cy Young Award winner in 1957.

■ 42 JACKIE ROBINSON

As the man who integrated major league baseball in 1947, Jackie Robinson holds an esteemed place in the game's history. It should also be noted, however, that he was a fabulous ballplayer who compiled a .311 career batting average in 10 seasons ('47-

Robinson (l) with Sam Jethroe, who broke the Braves color line.

56), winning the National League batting title in 1949 and being voted NL Rookie of the Year in '47 and the league's MVP in '49. A native of Cairo, Georgia, Robinson never played for the Braves, spending his entire career with the Brooklyn Dodgers. On the observance of the 50th anniversary of his big league debut, which came against the Boston Braves, Major League Baseball requested that all teams retire No. 42 in the Hall of Famer's honor. Thus, the Braves added Robinson's number to Monument Grove.

■ 41 EDDIE MATHEWS

The only Brave to play for the franchise in Boston, Milwaukee and Atlanta, Eddie Mathews was one of the greatest third basemen of all time and one of the game's most feared left-handed sluggers. His 512 career home runs rank 12th on the all-time list, and Willie McCovey is the only National Leaguer to hit more homers from the left side of the plate than Mathews. In 1953, the Braves' first season in Milwaukee, he led the majors with 47 home runs at age 21. Mathews hit a 10th-inning home run to win Game 4 of the 1957 World Series, and Milwaukee went on to beat the heavily favored Yankees in seven games. He and Hank Aaron combined for 863 home runs as teammates, a major league record. Mathews' 135 RBIs in 1953 still rank as the modern franchise record. He also managed the team from late 1972 to late 1974.

▮ 44 HANK AARON

ATLANTA BRAVES

Perhaps the greatest player of all time and certainly the greatest Brave ever, Hank Aaron hit 733 of his record 755 career home runs with the club from 1954-1974. He's best known for hitting his 715th home run on April 8, 1974, to break Babe Ruth's lifetime record. However, "Hammerin' Hank" was much more than a slugger. He was a superb all-around outfielder who won two batting titles and four Gold Gloves and stole 20 or more bases six times to go along with four home run championships and an incomparable list of offensive records. No other player in the game's history was as consistent as Aaron was over such an extended period of time. For instance, he had a major league record 15 seasons of 30 or more home runs. In 1957, he was named the National League MVP and batted .393 in the World Series victory over the Yankees. In 23 seasons in the majors, he made the All-Star team in all but his first and last year.

▮ 35 PHIL NIEKRO

ATLANTA BRAVES

The latest Brave to be inducted into the National Baseball Hall of Fame, an honor that came in Turner Field's inaugural season, Phil Niekro won 318 career games — 268 as a Brave from 1964-83. A master of the rare and elusive knuckleball, he pitched the Braves' first no-hitter in Atlanta, beating San Diego, 9-0, on August 5, 1973. He helped the Braves win division titles in 1969 and '82. In 1967, he led the National League with what was then a franchise-record 1.87 ERA. Niekro had three seasons of 20 or more victories and established numerous club records. In seven seasons from 1974-80, he led the league in innings four times and never finished out of the top five. In 1982, at age 43, he was 17-4 for a major league-best .810 winning percentage. An intense competitor, he won five Gold Gloves for defensive excellence. He teamed with his younger brother Joe for a major league-record 539 victories.

▮ 3 DALE MURPHY

ATLANTA BRAVEW

One of the most beloved and respected men ever to play major league baseball, Murphy is the only one of the five Braves with retired numbers not enshrined in the National Baseball Hall of Fame. However, he's not eligible until 1998. With 398 career home runs (371 as a Brave) and back-to-back National League MVP Awards (1982-83), he's certainly a legitimate candidate for Cooperstown. Primarily an outfielder with Atlanta from 1976-90, the reverent and gentlemanly Murphy strung together four consecutive seasons of at least 36 home runs and 100 RBIs from 1982-85 and had a career-high 44 home runs in 1987. He played in 740 consecutive games — 12th all-time — through July 9, 1986, the longest streak among active players at the time and one that has since been passed only by Cal Ripken Jr.

THE MONUMENTS

HANK AARON BUST

For years, the bust of Hank Aaron greeted fans on the Field Level concourse at Atlanta-Fulton County Stadium before it was moved to Turner Field. The head-and-shoulders likeness is accompanied by a plaque that reads: "Presented to The City of Atlanta. In Commemoration of the Outstanding Contributions of Henry Louis Aaron to the game of Baseball and to this City. The Citizens & Southern National Bank. The Georgia Marble Company."

HANK AARON STATUE

The idea to erect a statue of the all-time home run king at Atlanta-Fulton County Stadium came from

ALLISON SHIRREFFS

former Braves public relations director Bob Hope and former Braves pitcher Pat Jarvis. But by the time the bronze sculpture was unveiled a month after Hank Aaron's induction into the National Baseball Hall of Fame in 1982, it had become a true community project.

Hundreds of citizens made contributions to the project. And among the many recognizable names on the donor list were: Felipe Alou, Dusty Baker, Tony Cloninger, Ralph Garr, Bob Gibson, Milo Hamilton, Bob Horner, Dave Johnson, Ernie Johnson, Stan Kasten, Bowie Kuhn, Denny Lemaster, the Los Angeles Dodgers, Dale Murphy, Phil Niekro, Burt Reynolds, Warren Spahn, Joe Torre, Flip Wilson and Andrew Young.

The dedication of the statue by Denver sculptor Ed Dwight was to coincide with Aaron's induction at Cooperstown, but delays in the fund-raising process pushed it back a month to September 7.

The statue itself is nine feet tall and weighs 2,800 pounds. It cost $85,000 and depicts Aaron in his follow-through after hitting career home run No. 715, breaking Babe Ruth's all-time record on April 8, 1974.

TY COBB STATUE

Known as the "Georgia Peach" because he hailed from Royston in northeast Georgia, Ty Cobb never played for the Braves nor was he associated with the franchise in any way. But considering his accomplishments in baseball and his status as a famous Georgian, the presence of his statue at Atlanta-Fulton County Stadium and now Turner Field certainly is appropriate.

Its inscription offers succinct testimony to the man it honors: "Tyrus Raymond Cobb. 1886-1961. Known as the Georgia Peach. Charter Member of Baseball Hall of Fame. Leading Batsman of all Major

League History. .367 Average, 4,191 Hits."

Though Pete Rose has since passed Cobb in career hits, the legend of the Georgia Peach is firmly entrenched in baseball history. The statue, crafted in 1976 by Austrian sculptor Felix deWeldon, shows the ever-aggressive Cobb sliding into third base past another Hall of Famer, Frank "Home Run" Baker.

It was commissioned by Mills Lane of C&S Bank, who was instrumental in building the stadium and luring the Braves to Atlanta from Milwaukee.

JANICE E. RETTALIATA

PHIL NIEKRO STATUE

To this day, Phil Niekro sounds as amazed as he and everyone else was back in 1985 when Ted Turner commissioned a statue in his honor. Not that "Knucksie" wasn't deserving, it's just that

Turner's sense of timing was . . . well, peculiar, to say the least. After all, Niekro was not only alive and well, but also pitching very effectively in the American League.

"I was puzzled why it would go up," said Niekro, who became the first active big leaguer to have a statue erected in his honor at a major league stadium. "I had left Atlanta. I wasn't in the Hall of Fame. And I wasn't near the status of Henry Aaron and Ty Cobb. I wasn't even in the same ballpark or league with their careers. But it was there, and I don't think too many would turn it down."

Of course, now the statue of the great knuckleball pitcher looks quite appropriate at Turner Field, especially with his Hall of Fame induction taking place in the new ballpark's first summer.

The statue was funded almost entirely by Turner, who has always been a great admirer of Niekro, one of the most popular players in franchise history. Denver sculptor Ed Dwight, who created the Aaron statue, also produced the Niekro memorial. The cost was $130,000, about $30,000 of which came from the general public and the rest from the Braves and Turner.

The Braves 400 Club donated the plaque that reads: Phil "Knucksie" Niekro. Five times an All-Star, Phil was always an All-Star to Atlanta and baseball fans everywhere. He won 318 games in a 24-year major league career, including a 9-0 no-hit victory at Atlanta-Fulton County Stadium on August 5, 1973. He struck out 3,342 batters in 864 games. Led NL in games started 4 times, in complete games 4 times, and in victories twice. Phil and brother Joe, the winningest brothers in major league history, won a combined record total 539 ML games.

The text concludes with these words from Phil: "There's no better Braves fan anywhere than I."

KYLE CHRISTY

Atlanta Mayor Bill Campbell (l) assists Ivan Allen, Jr., in cutting the ribbon to open the Braves museum named after the former mayor. Hank Aaron and Braves chairman Bill Bartholomay (r) applaud their work.

A STROLL THROUGH HISTORY

It would be convenient to regard 1966, the year the Braves moved to Atlanta, as the beginning of the franchise's history. Indeed, there are those who do so. But ignoring the Braves' roots in Boston and Milwaukee is like beginning the study of American history at the end of the Civil War. Who cares about the Declaration of Independence and the Constitution anyway!

Indeed, if you don't care to know about incredible men such as Harry Wright, George Stallings, Rabbit Maranville, Wally Berger, Tommy Holmes, Sam Jethroe, Joe Adcock, Warren Spahn and many more, then pretend the Braves were born in Atlanta. Fortunately, the Braves didn't do that when they worked with the Atlanta History Center to develop the Ivan Allen Jr. Braves Museum and Hall of Fame at Turner Field.

And because they chose to tell the whole story of this extraordinarily colorful franchise, visitors to Turner Field have the chance to absorb some of the richest baseball history this side of Cooperstown (or any side, for that matter).

Named after the former Atlanta mayor who led the campaign to build Atlanta Stadium and lure the Braves to the South, the museum's storyline starts with the birth of the franchise in 1871 and continues right up to the thrilling 1990s. The 4,000-square-foot facility has a distinct baseball flavor with its green-and-wood decor. Located behind the left-field stands, it entertains fans as it educates them about the oldest continuously operating professional sports franchise in America.

Yes, the Braves — playing under several nicknames in three cities — have been on the field, without interruption, longer than any other team in pro

The Boston section of the museum gives fans the perspective of being an outfielder at the old South End Grounds.

baseball. And thanks to the Braves and the Atlanta History Center's Ted Ryan, who spearheaded the evolution of the museum, this story springs to life through the use of some 200-plus artifacts, as well as video and audio presentations, all brought together in three vignettes representing the three cities the club has called home.

"It turned out better than I ever thought it would," Ryan said proudly. "It's my baby, but it took two and a half years instead of nine months."

Ryan visited the National Baseball Hall of Fame and Museum in Cooperstown, New York, as well as the only two other such baseball team museums, the St. Louis Cardinals' and the Texas Rangers', and the New England Sports Museum in Cambridge, Massachusetts, to study how to do such a project. He said he then used the book *The Braves Encyclopedia* as the basis for writing the storyline.

Ted Ryan enjoys the view from the museum's railroad car.

Before the advent of air travel, the Braves toured the National League in a sleeper car similar to the one at Turner Field.

Visitors entering the museum from the street entrance on the north side of Turner Field first encounter the Boston vignette and progress to Milwaukee and Atlanta. Fans coming in through the ballpark entrance are greeted by the Atlanta vignette and proceed in reverse chronological order.

The hub of the Boston section is a two-wall mural of the South End Grounds, the Braves' first permanent home and one that served them from 1871 into 1915. The mural allows visitors to enjoy the perspective of an outfielder standing in the old park, looking in at the only double-decked grandstand ever used by a major league club in Boston and one that was adorned by six distinctive spires.

The focus of the Milwaukee section is half of an actual railroad sleeper car that is one of the most unique aspects of the entire ballpark. Ryan decided on using it because Hank Aaron said in his book, *I Had a Hammer*, that the only place he felt socially integrated with his Braves teammates in the '50s was on the trains they traveled in from city to city and that it was there that he received his early education as a major leaguer.

The bat and ball from No. 715 are on permanent display for the first time.

Five authentic lockers display uniforms and various other artifacts.

By walking through the car, museum visitors not only can see how the Braves used to get around the National League before the advent of air travel, but they also can imagine what it would have been like to rub elbows with Milwaukee greats such as Hall of Famers Aaron, Spahn and Eddie Mathews. The voices of Aaron and Ernie Johnson, the former Milwaukee pitcher who became a popular broadcaster in Atlanta, fill the train with a warm recorded narrative about baseball on the rails.

Tracking down an authentic 1950s sleeper car was one thing; getting the 38,000-pound car into Turner Field was yet another.

"We got the train from John Ott, who used to be the director of the Atlanta History Center and now runs the B&O Railroad Museum in Baltimore," Ryan said. "Then, in order to get it in here, we had to sink the floor two and a half inches and reinforce the concrete slab from six inches to 18 inches. We installed

rails 30 feet out into the plaza. A crane lifted it off a truck and onto the tracks, then we used a backhoe to push it into the museum.

"It cleared the wall by about an inch and a half and the steel beam overhead by about the same. When it dropped the two and a half inches onto the tracks, it made a huge thump and everything shook.

"I saw two things stop construction workers in their tracks — when they flew in the foul polls by helicopter and when we brought in the train."

The Atlanta vignette is built around the Braves' dugout from Atlanta-Fulton County Stadium, a concept attributed to Rick Beard, executive director of the non-profit Atlanta History Center. Fans can sit on the actual bench the players used during the 1995 World Series. They can pick up the telephone Bobby Cox and Leo Mazzone used to call the bullpen and can see the Braves' bat rack and helmet rack from the old park.

PARTIAL LIST OF ARTIFACTS
ON DISPLAY OPENING NIGHT

BOSTON ERA (1871-1952)

- Harry Wright's 1871 scorebook.
- George Wright's lifetime National League pass.
- Boston Red Stockings 1871 lapel pin.
- Catcher's masks, circa 1895 and 1910.
- Town ball bat, circa 1870.
- Lemon peel baseball, 1871.
- Les Mann's 1914 "Miracle" Braves warm-up jacket.
- Spalding baseball used in 1914 World Series.
- Braves Field bench.
- Walton Cruise's sunglasses and uniform, circa 1921.

- "Milkman" Jim Turner's 1937 road uniform and rosin bag.
- Braves 1946 satin uniform.

MILWAUKEE ERA (1953-65)

- Hank Aaron rookie baseball card, 1954.
- Warren Spahn's 1963 jersey.
- Eddie Mathews' 1963 jersey.
- Hartland statues of Aaron, Spahn and Mathews.
- Ernie Johnson's 1957 warm-up jacket, glove and cap from 1957 World Series.
- 1957 World Champions ring and commemorative bat.
- Bob Rush's 1958 World Series uniform.

- Telegrams and correspondence relating to Hank Aaron's signing with the Braves.

ATLANTA ERA (1966-PRESENT)

- Ticket and program from Opening Day, 1966.
- Bat used by Hank Aaron to hit No. 715.
- Ball Aaron used to hit No. 715.
- Third base from the night Aaron hit No. 715.
- Part of the "Channel 17" jersey worn by Andy Messersmith in 1976.
- Jerseys, caps and other items worn by Dale Murphy, Bob Horner, Joe Torre, Darrell Evans and Tommie Aaron.
- The bat used by Bob Horner (Gary Matthews model) to hit a home run in his first professional game, 1978.
- WTBS microphone.
- Knee brace worn by Sid Bream during his famous slide to win the '92 NLCS.
- Tom Glavine's 1991 Cy Young Award.
- Fred McGriff's MVP trophy from the 1994 All-Star Game.
- Various items used by Glavine, Greg Maddux, David Justice, McGriff and other Braves during the '90s.

A 1946 satin jersey.

Andy Messersmith's 1976 jersey.

Scout's Alley includes these sequential pictures of Phil Niekro pitching as a high school sophomore.

The Atlanta section also includes five actual lockers — including that of Aaron, which contains the bat he used and the ball he hit for No. 715 to become the all-time home run king in 1974. It's the first time the bat and ball, which were locked in a bank vault for years until Aaron loaned them to the museum, have been on permanent display. The '95 World Series trophy, the four National League championship trophies, and replicas of the four championship rings the team has won this decade are on display, too.

Watching fans stroll through the exhibits is a treat in itself.

"People love it," Ryan said. "I've even had a couple tell me they got a little teary-eyed."

But Braves fans take their baseball seriously, so they've also offered a few suggestions. Ryan said two young girls from Louisiana, obviously Javier Lopez fans, were a bit miffed to find that David Justice's jersey was hung in one of the lockers so that it overlapped, and thus obscured, the name on their hero's jersey.

Then there was the older woman who, when she saw how the players' spikes had chewed up the Braves' bench, asked, "Why do they let them put their feet up in the dugout?" When Ryan explained that players liked to sit up on the back of the bench to get a better view of the field, she responded, "Well, it's not a nice habit. They shouldn't let them do that."

Ah, baseball, it's the little things that make it so great and the little details that make the Ivan Allen Jr. Braves Museum a delightful experience for all fans, young or old, serious or casual.

SCOUT'S ALLEY

Turner Field would have been a great ballpark even if it had been built without Scout's Alley . . . but

Fans can inspect bats or read scouting reports (l) or test their leaping skill against Otis Nixon's (r).

thank goodness it wasn't.

As many wonderful amenities as there are at the new Home of the Braves, there is nothing as original and unique as the area under the left-field stands that pays tribute to the men who scour the sandlots of America and many other parts of the world, literally searching for a needle in a haystack — a ballplayer capable of developing into a big leaguer.

But Scout's Alley doesn't simply exist to credit the work of scouts. It also uses a combination of mural-like reproductions of actual scouting reports of popular Braves, along with interactive displays, games of skill, and computerized informational kiosks to provide fans a chance to learn what it takes to make the grade in baseball.

Of the many compelling sights in Scout's Alley,

perhaps none is as irresistible as the photos taken May 1, 1955, of Phil Niekro as a sophomore pitcher at Bridgeport (Ohio) High School.

Located just inside the plaza entrance to Scout's Alley on the right wall, they're part of the "How They Scout" display. Contributed by Niekro from his personal collection, one life-size blowup shows him demonstrating his famous knuckleball grip, just as he did for photographers hundreds of times in his Hall of Fame career. But even better is a six-shot sequence of his pitching motion, from windup to delivery.

The photos provide the type of rare flashback to a major leaguer's childhood that you seldom see, especially of a player of Niekro's stature and with pictures of such quality.

Both walls of Scout's Alley are lined with blown-up

The batting cages allow hitters to show their form to amateur "scouts" who size up the prospective talent.

photos of 10 famous Braves, past and present. These are included with the actual scouting reports filed on the players when they were in high school. The players featured are: John Smoltz, Mark Lemke, Chipper Jones, Dale Murphy, Hank Aaron and Greg Maddux, Rico Carty, Tom Glavine, Steve Bedrosian and Niekro.

Additionally, some 200 more scouting reports (roughly 50 of the players featured played for the Braves during their careers) can be accessed via three interactive kiosks that have several other features, including a baseball trivia game.

To make Scout's Alley literally come alive and to help fans appreciate the skill it takes to play professional baseball at the highest level, the interactive exhibits and batting and pitching games were included.

There are six interactive displays, dealing with various facets of hitting, pitching and fielding, on the ballpark side of Scout's Alley. One invites fans to test their jumping ability against the celebrated 11-foot leap Otis Nixon made — known simply as "The Catch" — on July 25, 1992, to rob Pittsburgh's Andy Van Slyke of a home run and preserve the Braves' 13-game winning streak.

Another interactive allows fans to compare bats used by Babe Ruth (40 ounces/36 inches), Aaron (33/35), Murphy (33/35) and Chipper Jones (32/34 left-handed and 32 1/2/35 right-handed).

The other exhibits demonstrate: Maddux's various pitches; how to locate the "sweet spot" on a bat (the spot on the barrel that doesn't vibrate when it hits the ball); the types of gloves used by players at dif-

Children get to run from home plate to first base at Sky Field.

ALLISON SHIRREFFS

ferent positions; and where in the strike zone Aaron most liked to hit the ball.

Batting and pitching cages round out Scout's Alley. They not only allow fans to test the speed and accuracy of their throws and their hitting prowess, but they do so with a colorful Braves theme. "Aaron Hits 715" reads the backdrop in one cage that includes a painting of the all-time home run king. And "Braves Take World Series" is the theme of another cage in which the backdrop has a painting of David Justice, the home run hero in Game Six of the '95 Series.

For those who may not be up for an athletic test or who just want to see what it would be like to be Skip Caray or Pete Van Wieren, there's the Fantasy Play-By-Play booth. Broadcaster wannabes can call the action of a great moment in Braves history or narrate an inning of the game in progress and take home a tape of their Turner Field audition.

Scout's Alley is a one-of-its-kind original and, perhaps more than any other feature at the new Home of the Braves, makes Turner Field the rarest of diamonds.

SKY FIELD $1 MILLION HOME RUN RULES

■ The prize of $1 million will be paid in increments of $50,000 over 20 years, without interest.

■ No equipment or tools can be used to catch or retrieve the ball, except for baseball gloves no larger than official major league size.

■ No winner will be declared and the promotion continues if:

• The ball rolls or bounces out of Sky Field.

• The ball is not recoverable.

• The ball lands in a non-public area of Sky Field.

• The ball touches a person or object (other than the foul pole) outside of Sky Field before entering it.

• The ball wouldn't have entered Sky Field if not for use of impermissible equipment.

• The ball is caught by a person using impermissible equipment.

■ A person may be disqualified for using unsportsmanlike conduct, including physical force, to retrieve the ball, and the prize can be awarded to another person who, in the opinion of judges, would have caught or retrieved the ball.

■ The $1 million will be awarded to charity if the person who caught the ball used unsportsmanlike behavior and no alternate can be determined; or if it is impossible for the judges to determine the official winner.

NOTE: Four video cameras record all activity at Sky Field.

LOOK . . . UP IN THE SKY . . . IT'S . . . SKY FIELD

It rises off Turner Field's left-field roof like a gigantic sporting goods store reaching for the heavens. It contains literally thousands of baseballs and hundreds of bats, not to mention dozens of gloves, bases, batting helmets and assorted other authentic Braves baseball equipment straight from the clubhouse. Of course, it's not a baseball outlet store or even a warehouse for Braves gear; it's a 42-foot-high pop art structure and a monument to baseball and soda pop, not necessarily in that order.

The giant, fireworks-spewing contour bottle is only one of many unique features of Coca-Cola Sky Field, but it is definitely the most distinctive and the most noticeable from all areas of Turner Field.

This first-of-its-kind creation of the Atlanta-based soft drink giant covers 23,000 square feet and includes such things as:

■ A pitcher's mound, a regulation 90-foot basepath, home plate and first base on a natural grass and dirt "field."

■ A radio broadcast booth built into the base of the bottle.

■ A "dugout" with a bench and bat racks.

■ Nine 28-foot-tall baseball "cards" featuring action pictograms of players.

BOTTLE STATS

THE COCA-COLA CONTOUR BOTTLE AT SKY FIELD IS 42 FEET TALL AND IS DECORATED WITH:

■ 6,680 baseballs
■ 60 baseball shoes
■ 64 bases
■ 48 batting helmets
■ 18 catcher's mitts
■ 290 bats and bat ends

■ 86 fielder's gloves
■ 24 jerseys
■ 71 catcher's masks
■ 16 chest protectors
■ 24 pitching rubbers

THE COCA-COLA SIGN ON THE BOTTLE IS MADE OF:

■ 2,000 Coke cans
■ 2,000 bottle caps

■ 118 strobe lights
■ 200 feet of neon

ALLISON SHIRREFFS

■ Air vapor "refreshers" (cool zones) that fans can walk under to cool off.

■ Cannons shaped like Coke bottles that shoot streamers into the stands after Braves home runs.

Sky Field became an immediate hit with fans as soon as it opened May 29, 1997. Youngsters line up to run from home plate to first base, and everyone comes to enjoy a skyline view of Braves games on one side and downtown Atlanta on the other.

"Baseball is not an intense game," says Steve Koonin, vice-president of sports marketing for Coca-Cola. "It's a sociable game. Our research shows that people want to have fun. We think we have something that will give the fans more entertainment."

Many fans also come with their baseball gloves in hope of making a $1-million catch.

Though chances are remote of a fair ball reaching Sky Field during any given game — if ever — the huge $1-million check hanging on a wall next to the contour bottle reminds fans of the reward The Coca-Cola Company will pay to the person who catches or retrieves the first home run ball hit into the attraction.

Since Sky Field is 435 feet from home plate and 80 feet above the field, it would take a mammoth blast with a trajectory capable of carrying the ball over 500 feet to reach the 50-foot-wide target zone. However,

The Braves Clubhouse Store allows fans to practice the "sport" of shopping.

ATLANTA BRAVES

home runs of that distance, though few and far between, have been hit. New St. Louis slugger Mark McGwire thrilled fans in early August with a near-Sky Field experience, a batting practice shot that hit five feet from the top of the left-field foul pole.

Thus, standing in wait at Sky Field is akin to playing a baseball lottery, only better. There's no charge for entering and you don't have to wait until the 11 o'clock news to find out if you've won.

A CHOPPER'S PARADISE

"They came, they saw, they bought."

If a typical fan's visit to Turner Field can be summed up in six words, the above half-dozen might do it.

Or maybe, "Watch a game, buy some souvenirs."

After all, what's a Braves game without a memento? And at Turner Field, the place to shop for that keepsake is the 3,000-square-foot Braves Clubhouse Store located in the midst of the plaza, directly under the Big Ball.

If you want a foam tomahawk, a Braves cap or T-shirt, a Turner Field lapel pin, a Javier Lopez photo button, or a copy of *Chop Talk*, the team's official monthly magazine, you can find it in the Clubhouse Store. But that's only the beginning. You also can find Turner Field postcards, a backpack that looks like a bear dressed as a Brave, and pet collars and leads bearing the team's insignia.

In all, there are some 3,200 different items for sale in the store. Almost all of them — at least 3,000 — have "Braves" on them, according to Gary Morrow, retail general manager for Aramark, the ballpark's concessionaire.

Morrow estimates that somewhere in the neighborhood of 10,000 fans (almost one in four) pass through the Braves Clubhouse Store during the average game. Not all buy something, of course, but most do. He says the store averages between 6,000 and 8,000 transactions per game.

"It's far beyond what we expected," Morrow said. "The response from the fans has been fantastic . . . phenomenal. I've never seen anything like it."

Almost as soon as the gates to the plaza open three hours before game time, the onslaught begins. Within an hour, the store is crowded. It tapers off as game time approaches, but after two or three innings, there's steady traffic poring over the 29 different T-shirts, posters, pictures, and custom key chains. During the last couple of innings, the place gets packed again. But when the game ends . . . look out! You'd think it was the day after Thanksgiving at the mall. Fans absolutely swarm into the store looking for something to take home or a gift for a relative or friend.

Morrow said Turner Field commemorative merchandise has been a top seller. He stocks roughly 32 Turner Field items, ranging from the commemorative "First Game" program from April 4 to pewter lapel pins, jackets, T-shirts, polo shirts, patches, mugs, a 755 Hank Aaron Drive street sign, and even refrigerator magnets.

The best-selling item at the Clubhouse Store?

"Foam tomahawks," Morrow said, "and replica caps are second."

What else is hot? Anything with "Chipper Jones" on it, including the third baseman's candy bar.

At Turner Field, fans don't shop until they drop. They just shop until the Clubhouse Store is locked up an hour after the last out.

RECIPE FOR SUCCESS

It's funny how things work out sometimes. In the blink of an eye, the worst team in baseball in 1990

Fans enjoy watching games while lining the railing along the upper level of the Chop House.

<small>MAX ANTON BIRNKAMMER</small>

<small>ALLISON SHIRREFFS</small>

Braves baseball and barbecue, a perfect combination.

becomes the best team of record over the ensuing seven years. A lowly 25th-round draft pick named Mark Lemke becomes a regular post-season god. And a "last-minute" component of Turner Field becomes the single biggest sensation of the Braves' dazzling new home.

"In the restaurant business, if you turn over your tables two or three times (for a meal), you're considered a smash," said Braves president Stan Kasten midway through the '97 season. "At the Chop House, we're turning it over five to seven times a night!"

And that's not just occasionally — that's every night.

"Actually, we're turning it over as many as nine times a night," said Scott Huey, executive chef at Turner Field and the man whose barbecue is the main attraction at the two-level, open-air restaurant in right field.

Huey's original projection was to serve 150,000 pounds of pork barbecue in Turner Field's first season. By mid-season, he'd already dished out 160,000 pounds, causing him to double his original estimate.

"You never could have found someone four years ago who would have said we'd be serving the amount of barbecue we are," said Janet Marie Smith, the Braves' vice-president of development. "There are formulas for everything we do and how we should do them in this business. No formula ever would have gotten you to the Chop House. The quantitative and qualitative approach to architecture never showed that."

Yet because the Braves felt a restaurant was a more appropriate family amenity for their ballpark than the "brew pub" that was originally planned, the Chop House sprang to life in right-center field. A true "first" for a major league ballpark, it gives all fans the opportunity to watch the game live from two levels while feasting on Chef Huey's barbecue and numerous other selections.

Like everything else at Turner Field, the Chop House has a complete baseball theme. Besides affording customers an excellent view of the playing field, the restaurant's decor includes an overhead Braves schedule on the first level where a large 'W' or smaller 'L' is added after every game so you can monitor the team's streaks while you polish off your Thai Cobb salad. Each major league team is represented by its cap behind the bar in a display arranged by league and division.

Lower-level tables sport the Braves' tomahawk logo, and upper-level picnic tables are shaded by bright yellow umbrellas that provide a refreshing touch of color to the park.

The way fans flocked to the Chop House thrilled everyone associated with the Braves, but none more

than Huey. A 33-year-old native of Young Harris in north Georgia, he's a long-time Braves fan who regards catering to the team's fans as his "dream job."

Just as the huge blowup of Hank Aaron's 715th home run ball and the flashing neon tomahawk on top of the scoreboard are Turner Field signatures, so too is Huey's personal-blend barbecue sauce. He and his staff prepare 200 gallons of it for each game, and it may be the only recipe in Atlanta that's even more guarded than the original formula for Coca-Cola.

"I've been around barbecue all my life. This is an old recipe of my dad's that I've tweaked. I spent 120 hours developing it, and I'm the only one who knows all 25 ingredients," said Huey, who learned to cook from his mother and grandmother but has since schooled at the Culinary Institute of America and has studied under some of the finest chefs in Europe and America.

"The recipe is on a master file, but I deleted four ingredients. The kitchen puts it together, then calls me to add the final four ingredients. There are six vinegars in the sauce, and I'm the only one who knows what four of those are."

Huey smokes his hams in a custom-built, cast-iron smoker that's so large it won't fit in the Chop House kitchen. Consequently, it resides in the media parking lot on the southeast side of the ballpark. It weighs 6,000 pounds, and Huey believes it's the largest ever built for a retail operation.

And during a homestand, it doesn't get much time to cool off.

"You know you've got a pretty successful restaurant when people don't mind lining up and waiting an hour and a half for a seat," said Huey.

How often?

"Every night."

And to think, Turner Field was almost built without it.

'BUY ME SOME PAN-FRIED TROUT AND BANANAS FOSTER . . .'

There are a lot of ways to watch the Braves at Turner Field, none more exquisite than doing so from the 755 Club in left field. If there's ever been a truly elegant place to spend a night at the ballpark, this is it.

It's not hot dogs, peanuts and Cracker Jacks. It's pan-fried Georgia mountain trout, carved steamship round, cooked-to-order pasta, the freshest vegetables, and an astonishing dessert bar. It's not for everyone. But fans there can (and do) root, root, root for the home team, just as they can from the grandstand, the Chop House or Coca-Cola Sky Field.

One of Turner Field's many tributes to Hank Aaron, the private club's name comes from the all-time home run king's career home run total. Members of the club can dine in either the posh indoor setting where only a wall of floor-to-ceiling glass separates them from the chopping and chanti-ng, or outside on the two-tiered Terrace Bistro. Both afford a dazzling view from the Club Level of the ballpark. There's also the indoor Sports Bar where there are enough televisions to keep fans in touch with the Braves and everything else going on in baseball.

Like everything else at Turner Field, the 500-seat 755 Club is unmistakably themed for Braves baseball. Large, framed photographs of memorable players line the back wall. The greats, as well as the nearly greats, are represented, ranging from Dale Murphy, Joe Torre, Ralph Garr, Dusty Baker, Darrell Evans, Bob Horner and Fred McGriff to Mike Lum, Zane Smith, Claudell Washington, Rafael Ramirez and Preston Hanna. As is appropriate, however, the photographic highlight features Henry Louis Aaron. A sequence of five large, black-and-white pictures shows "The Hammer's" whip-action swing from beginning to end as a young Milwaukee Brave.

The spacious main dining room has two levels,

Some fans prefer to dine outdoors at the 755 Club's Bistro.

MAX ANTON BIRNKAMMER

Executive chef Scott Huey serves a fresh buffet at the 755 Club that's second to none.

and appointments include high-backed leather lounge seats, live plants, white-linen tablecloths and napkins, and white china bearing the 755 Club logo. There are televisions in every direction, including a bank of 16 spaced every eight feet along the front wall.

Gold-medal-winning Turner Field executive chef Scott Huey specializes in 19th century traditional Southern cuisine, and he spares no effort in presenting buffets with seemingly endless selections that are scrumptious to all the culinary senses.

His boundless list of offerings includes such creations as:

▮ Rack of elk with wild berry chutney.

▮ Stuffed rack of wild boar with blueberry chutney.

▮ American bison New York strip steak with three pepper sauce.

▮ Broiled red snapper with lemon pepper butter and sauteed plantains and peppers.

▮ A brace of grilled marinated quail with Cilantro sauce.

▮ Cornmeal Southern fried chicken.

At a ballpark?

Yes, but not just at any ballpark.

The Bistro, located just in front of the 755 Club's main dining room glass windows, brightens the look of the ballpark's outfield with its red and yellow chairs, though white linen still dresses the tables.

The dining room is adjoined by a banquet room for business meetings, private parties and major social events and receptions. During Braves games, the club is open only to members, but on non-game days, non-members may reserve it for functions.

In case you're wondering, "upside of casual" is

considered proper dress for the Club during Braves games. That, naturally, would include the special line of 755 Club merchandise — caps, shirts, sweatshirts, etc. — available there.

The 755 Club opened in the midst of Turner Field's inaugural season, July 10 to be exact. Membership for the first year (through February 28, 1998) was $250. Future memberships will run March-February.

A distinctive addition to Braves baseball, the 755 Club is yet another feature that makes Turner Field such a unique facility.

SIGHTS 'N' SOUNDS

The game-day personality of Turner Field is shaped by many factors, perhaps none as powerful as the combined impact of the ballpark's scoreboards and sound system.

Think about it . . . What would a Braves game be like without the music, P.A. announcements, replays, messages and all the other information — like the score and the count — that's constantly filling the eyes and ears of thousands of fans? Thanks to the video board in the plaza, the images begin even

Jennifer Berger at Turner Field's scoreboard controls.

before you enter the park, and they continue as you're leaving.

All those sights and sounds that mold the overall environment of Turner Field are the responsibility of Jennifer Berger, the Braves' 30-year-old director of audio-video operations and a serious, life-long baseball fan.

"Our main goal is to create a fun and family-oriented atmosphere in the ballpark," said Berger, who oversees a staff of four full-time and 25 part-time, seasonal employees, including the public address announcer and the organist. "We want our programming to inform and entertain the fans but never to overshadow the game, only to enhance it."

What makes the Turner Field scoreboard operation particularly unique is that there are two distinctly different programs or "shows" going on all the time. The main show is on the 29-foot by 38-foot BravesVision video board and the accompanying 32-foot by 64-foot Daktronics matrix board in center field. Simultaneously, another program is shown in the plaza on the 16-foot, 6-inch by 22-foot video board and the 3-foot by 72-foot matrix board.

"What our show has that others don't have is we have two shows at one time," said Berger, who points out that the Panasonic video boards are among the brightest in sports. "The plaza side has its own video and matrix and a separate sound system. Because of that, we have double impact on the fans. It's our greatest challenge. That's very different than anywhere else in baseball. We're the only team in baseball with two video boards operating simultaneously with different programming."

The main scoreboard, naturally, is an integral part of a Braves game. Among many things, it displays lineups and pictures and statistics of players. Between innings, it allows the Braves and their sponsors to interact with the crowd in promotions such as the Junior Brave of the Game and the Cap

The "chopping" tomahawk logo above the scoreboard adds yet another distinctive touch to the ballpark.

Challenge, the latter being a takeoff on the old "hand-is-quicker-than-the-eye shell game" that never fails to entertain.

During the game, the plaza features the Braves' broadcast on its video board and the announcers on its sound system, in effect creating a massive family room where hundreds of fans often prefer to watch the game — just like they do at home — in front of the TV.

One of the most distinctive features of Turner Field sits atop the gigantic scoreboard complex and helps give the ballpark its captivating "Braves baseball" presence. That is the "Braves" logo sign and its neon tomahawk that can be activated to "chop" sequentially.

"It's a very unique accessory to the park, being able to 'chop' the neon tomahawk when the fans chant," Berger said. "The 'chop' is indigenous to the

Braves, and to be able to incorporate it and have movement in this element is great for the ballpark and our fans."

The combination of the video and matrix boards with the audio system can have a dramatic impact on the crowd. Berger's staff draws from a library of thousands of CDs with music and sound effects to embellish the mood of any given situation.

"We have a list of songs for each situation — pitching changes, when particular batters come up, a home run or a rally . . .," Berger said. "We try to keep the music as fresh and upbeat as possible and we try to please all our fans.

"We look at our demographics. On Friday nights, we get more young people, so we might play more rock music or progressive than on Saturday or Sunday afternoon when there are more families and

1997 TURNER FIELD BATTER INTRODUCTION SONGS
PLAYER / TITLE / ARTIST

Danny Bautista/Cold Rock A Party/MC Lyte

Rafael Belliard/Boom Boom Boom/Outhere Brothers

Mike Bielecki/*Zero/Smashing Pumpkins

Jeff Blauser/Dr. Feelgood/Motley Crue

Greg Colbrunn/New Sensation/INXS

Alan Embree/Get Ready For This/2 Unlimited

Chad Fox/Good Vibrations/Marky Mark

Tom Glavine/These Sounds Fall Into My Mind/
   Bucketheads

Tony Graffanino/Unchained/Van Halen

Andruw Jones/*Let Me Clear My Throat/DJ Kool

Chipper Jones/*Welcome To The Jungle/
   Guns N Roses

Ryan Klesko/*Evenflow/Pearl Jam

Mark Lemke/Hitman/AB Logic

Keith Lockhart/Unbelievable/EMF

Kenny Lofton 1/*Who You Wit/Jay Z

Kenny Lofton 2/*Mo Money Mo
Problems/Notorious B.I.G.

Javy Lopez 1/*Fonquete/Unknown

Javy Lopez 2/*Pumpin/Proyecto Uno

Greg Maddux/Song 2 (Woo HOO!)/Blur

Fred McGriff/*I'll Be Missing You/Puff Daddy

Kevin Millwood/Higher Ground/
   Red Hot Chili Peppers

Denny Neagle/Machinehead/Bush

Eddie Perez/*Latinos/Proyecto Uno

John Smoltz/More Human Than Human/
   White Zombie

Michael Tucker/*Can't Nobody Hold Me Down/
   Puff Daddy

Mark Wohlers/*Thunderstruck/AC/DC

* Selected by player

we play more oldies and music that appeals to kids. We work with the fans to cheer the team."

The entire production — in the ballpark and in the plaza — is directed by Berger and executed by 15 members of her staff who sit in a high-tech control room filled with switches, knobs, monitors and wires on the press level (first-base side) of Turner Field.

A graduate of Towson State, the Maryland school that also produced Braves general manager John Schuerholz, Berger is the Braves' first full-time audio-video director. She started her department from scratch, did the hiring, and created the programming — just as she did for the Colorado Rockies at Coors Field that opened in Denver in '95 and just as she assisted in doing for Baltimore's Oriole Park at Camden Yards that opened in '92.

"I grew up in Baltimore as a huge Orioles fan, but I never dreamed that I would have a career in baseball," said Berger, who started working with the Orioles as a college intern. "In college, I went to a game with some friends and we were talking about what we wanted to do. They (Orioles) played a real emotional video about Cal Ripken Jr., and I said, 'That's what I want to do, something creative that will really move people.' Two years later, I heard about the internship, and now I have the greatest job in sports. I love every second of it!"

And because she does, Braves fans love Turner Field all the more.

A SPECIAL PLACE
FOR SPECIAL FANS

They may not know what the infield fly rule is, understand the difference between a suicide squeeze bunt and a safety squeeze, or be able to articulate the difference between a curveball and a slider . . . but kids are the future of baseball. If

TOMMY BUTLER

Youngsters never know who they'll run into at Tooner Field.

they're to learn about the game and fall in love with it like generations before them, they need things to attract them to the ballpark and keep their attention once they arrive.

Hence, the Braves and the Cartoon Network created Tooner Field, home of the fictional Toonerville Sluggers and the favorite stopping place for countless Braves fans of the pint-sized variety.

Located behind the Chop House in the concourse under the right-field stands, Tooner Field is decorated, inside and out, with colorful murals of well-known cartoon characters in a baseball setting. Many of the characters such as Scooby Doo, Yogi Bear and Fred Flintstone, in fact, make live appearances in the air-conditioned area.

Designed and customized primarily for ages six through 11, but appealing to everyone from toddlers to seniors, Tooner Field also has tables and chairs and a concession counter built for the smaller set.

And the servings and prices of concessions are reduced, as well.

"The Braves wanted to have a specific area for kids, and what we came up with is a simple concept that's an entertaining and amusing and fun place kids want go to," said Bob Bryant, director of sports marketing for the Cartoon Network, a TBS subsidiary. "And because it's a kids' area, it translates into a family area.

"We wanted to go beyond just decorating the area, and we did that with the concept of the Toonerville Sluggers, banners for retired numbers, and selecting some characters to be spectators. We came up with creative designs that directly apply the image of our characters in a baseball setting."

Televisions throughout Tooner Field enable visitors to be entertained by cartoons before and after games but also to keep up with the Braves from the first pitch to the last.

Even Skip Caray (r) and Pete Van Wieren enjoy a visit to Monument Grove.

THE PEOPLE

THE VIEW FROM THE BOOTH

Skip Caray and Pete Van Wieren have been broadcasting Braves games for 22 years. Nothing against the first 21 at Atlanta-Fulton County Stadium, but they say there's no place like Turner Field for doing their jobs.

"It's great for us. Our booth is right behind the plate, so if we screw up now, we don't have any excuses," quipped Caray.

But, of course, Caray's fondness for Turner Field goes beyond being centered behind the plate as opposed to being off to the right or left — depending on whether he was working radio or TV — at Atlanta-Fulton County Stadium. That new parking space doesn't hurt.

"We have assigned parking spaces here," he pointed out. "We take 50 steps and we're in the park; 25 steps and we're in the locker room; 30 more and we're at the elevator; another 10 and you're in the booth. It's a real pleasure to come to work."

Van Wieren agreed.

"Getting from the field to the booth or from the booth to the field at the old stadium could take 10 to 15 minutes because of the layout," he said. "Here, everything is close. If you need to get down to the field quickly or up to the booth quickly, you can do it. And the two booths for radio and TV are side-by-side, which saves a lot of time when we're changing. The visiting broadcasters appreciate having their own booths for radio and TV, too, instead of having to share them like they did before. From a working standpoint, everything is 100 percent."

As important as the working conditions are for Caray and Van Wieren, their compliments for Turner Field extend much further.

"This is an elegant ballpark," Caray said. "The way you can see that big baseball when you're coming down Hank Aaron Drive, it's great. I think the fans are having more fun here, and the sight lines are excellent for baseball."

Van Wieren even goes so far as to compare Turner Field to one of the great sports edifices of all-time.

"The look, the feel of the place . . . everyone tries to compare it to other ballparks. The one it reminds me a little of is Yankee Stadium," he said. "It has the same look, the same shape, except there's not a lot of foul territory. But when I'm up here, it feels a lot like it did last October (1996) during the World Series at Yankee Stadium."

Hopefully, Turner Field will someday have a history as rich as that of "The House that Ruth Built." But in the meantime, Caray and Van Wieren say it will do just fine.

AN OUTSIDE VOICE

Rick Cerone as a broadcaster (above) and as a Braves catcher.

There probably aren't many people who have been to more ballparks across America than Rick Cerone has. Braves fans may remember Cerone as a back-up catcher in Atlanta during the 1985 season. That was just a relatively brief stop for him in an 18-year big league career in both leagues from 1975-92. Now as a broadcaster for CBS Radio and the Yankees, not to mention being a minor league club owner, he continues to make the rounds at all levels of professional baseball.

To say that Turner Field hit a home run with Cerone would be an understatement. A grand slam would be more accurate.

According to Cerone, Turner Field brings together all the best of spring training, minor league baseball, and the Boardwalk at the Jersey Shore and puts it together in a major league setting to provide fans an unequaled experience.

"I love it," said Cerone, who came to Atlanta to broadcast the Orioles-Braves game for CBS Radio on June 14.

"What I did was to go out the night before and experience the whole thing the way a fan would. The Braves thought of everything. I felt like I was at a big party. The way I described it on the radio was that I felt like I was at the Jersey Shore on the Boardwalk because there's so much to choose from."

Cerone owns the Wilmington Blue Rocks in the Class-A Carolina League and is constructing a new stadium in Newark, New Jersey, that will house his Newark Bears in 1998. As either a player or broadcaster, he's been to every major league park that's been in use over the past 23 years with the lone exception of Coors Field.

"Their first concern in building Turner Field obviously was kids . . . they wanted to be fan friendly and kids friendly," he said. "I was really, really impressed.

"I went to both levels of the Chop House. You could smell that barbecue everywhere — it was great — and the plaza out front with all those TV sets where you can watch every game! My two favorite things were Scout's Alley and going up to the left-field roof (Coca-Cola Sky Field).

"For a kid — even a big kid like me — to see the scouting reports on the players as they were coming up and all the interactive games and even the museum. That was my favorite thing. They've really taken the whole minor league experience and atmosphere and brought it to the big league level.

"Then all the things up on the roof — the big bottle with all the baseball equipment, the basepaths where the kids line up to run, the misting stations.

"It's beautiful, absolutely gorgeous. They really brought the kids into it. They've been doing that at the minor league level, and it's good to see the majors starting to do it. It's what baseball needs.

"The other thing I noticed is when pitchers are warming up, people can stand right above them and watch. It's a nice touch. It brings almost a spring training atmosphere to a big league game."

THE RANK AND FILE

SAM STOKES/GUEST RELATIONS SUPERVISOR

Sam Stokes started working Braves games as an usher at Aisle 301 of Atlanta Stadium in 1975. He's experienced a lot in 23 years at the ballpark, but nothing like what happened June 13 at Turner Field.

An elementary band teacher in the Atlanta school system, he's a saxophone player who's occasionally asked to play the national anthem before Braves games. That was the case when the Orioles came to Atlanta for the first interleague game in franchise history.

"I always play with my eyes closed," said Stokes, now supervisor of guest relations at Turner Field. "But this time, I heard a loud noise and it scared me to death, so I opened my eyes. I didn't know what it was. It was all the Orioles fans (loudly singing 'O's,' as is their tradition, instead of 'Oh' to start the anthem). It was exciting."

Stokes had grown quite attached to the old stadium and wondered how he'd like the new ballpark.

"I was over there for 22 years," he said, cocking his head in the direction of Atlanta-Fulton County Stadium. "But Turner Field is growing on me. A lot of fans are telling me how much they enjoy it here. They like being closer to the field, and they seem happier."

RAY WILLIAMS/USHER SUPERVISOR

Ray Williams has seen a few athletic facilities in his time, and he thinks Turner Field ranks at the top of the list.

In 1965, when the Crackers used Atlanta Stadium as their home while the Braves played their final season in Milwaukee, Williams was a supervisor of ushers — and he's been at it ever since, moving with the team to Turner Field. But he also crisscrossed the country for 40 years, officiating football and basketball games in more places than he can count.

"Of all the stadiums I've been to, and I've been to most, I feel this one is tops," Williams said. "It's a first-class field; it's very fan-oriented; people can bring their family and have a good time in a sports environment.

"The people who designed this did a great job for the fans. The old stadium was so compact, they'd just come in and go to their seats. There was the concourse, but the only thing there was food. Here there are so many other attractions. They don't have to stay in a compact area. They can walk around and meet friends. It's somewhat like an amusement park, but everything is baseball.

"If they don't want to sit, they can stand and watch and can go to several other areas. At Atlanta-Fulton County, if they got up, they missed a lot of the game. Here, they don't miss a thing."

WALTER BANKS/USHER

Walter Banks was born in 1939 when Atlanta's population was 300,000 and *Gone With The Wind* premiered. He started as an usher at Atlanta Stadium

J. STOLL

when it opened in 1965, was working Ted Turner's personal box when the old stadium closed, and retains that same responsibility at Turner Field.

Though some people may have had difficulty understanding the need for a new Home of the Braves, Banks was not one of them.

"I liked Atlanta-Fulton County, but you have to be proud that Atlanta is able to keep up with other cities by building a ballpark like this. You have to modernize," he said.

"Turner Field doesn't have to take a back seat to any stadium in the world. This is a first-class organization, and now we have a first-class stadium. It's progress.

"The old stadium served its purpose. It used to be the first in the South, but now there are others — Charlotte, Tampa. I remember when Birmingham and Atlanta used to be side by side and play each other in the Southern Association. Some people like things to stay the same, but Atlanta has a progressive attitude, and that's why it keeps moving ahead. Moving in here was like graduation, moving up to the next level."

Besides, Turner Field has given Banks — a veritable human fountain of facts and figures — an arsenal of new ammunition to delight the Turner Field fans who come his way.

"Fans ask me a lot of questions, and I like to be able to answer them," he said. "They ask me about the Coke bottle, and I tell them it's 42 feet tall, 435

feet away and 80 feet in the air, and that they used 2,000 Coke cans to decorate it."

Banks grins.

"I think Turner Field is beautiful."

SETTING THE TEMPO

Carolyn King Jones has gone from "worst to first" and from Atlanta-Fulton County Stadium to Turner Field. She's been a big part of Braves baseball almost as long as Tom Glavine, but even the best Braves fans wouldn't recognize her without her music.

It's Jones who can make the ballpark chop to life by playing "The Chant" on the Turner Field organ or who can soothe the crowd with "Take Me Out to the Ballgame" during the seventh-inning stretch. In fact, there are few things this side of a Braves victory that make a summer evening at the ballpark as enjoyable as the comforting tunes created by her fingertips.

"Ten years ago, the Braves ran an ad in the paper for an organist," said Jones, 27, who was a high school junior at the time. "My band teacher saw it and thought it would be a good idea if I tried out. My father took me and I got it."

She's been playing "Charge" and "Let's Go Braves" ever since. The lone exception came during a leave

TOMMY BUTLER

in 1996 when she delivered her daughter, Carmen Simone, who was considerate enough to wait to arrive until the Braves' long road trip during the Olympics.

Jones teaches music and art at

Briar Vista Elementary School in Atlanta. She studied piano but said she "took organ on the side." During Braves games, she plays entirely from memory, "for convenience" as much as anything, she said, because she improvises based on the game situation.

"My main objective is to cheer on the players and get the crowd involved," she said. "I try to help the players be at their best, and sometimes, it really works. When the crowd is into the game cheering, then we can tell it pumps up the players and it can get a good rally going."

Music has always been a family affair for Jones. Her father Fred King, who took her to the audition 10 years ago, played the guitar and other instruments when she and her brother, Fredrick, were growing up, thus helping to develop their interest. Fredrick is a music teacher at Cedar Grove Elementary School, and Carolyn's husband, Kevin Jones, is the band director at Druid Hills High School.

"He's a big help," Carolyn said of her husband. "He's a big sports fan. He comes to Braves games and tells me which songs sound the best, which orchestrations work, to use more bass here . . ."

Though she plays the same model pipe organ that was at Atlanta-Fulton County Stadium, Jones says everything sounds better at Turner Field.

"Turner Field is beautiful," she said. "The acoustics are much better, and all the new audio equipment helps the music and effects sound great. That makes it a lot nicer for me."

. . . And the fans.

THE VOICE IN THE SKY

Bill Bowers looks like a catcher, which he was, and sounds like . . . the great voice from beyond!

The booming, authoritative voice of Turner Field, Bowers debuted as the Braves' public address

TOMMY BUTLER

announcer the same day the new ballpark opened. He is the Braves' first new P.A. announcer in 30 years, taking over for Marshall Mann, who retired after the '96 season and died a short time later. The much-loved Mann had been the Braves' P.A. announcer since 1967.

Born in North Carolina and raised and schooled in Virginia, Bowers is a longtime Braves fan. A college catcher and slugger at Virginia Commonwealth, his career was cut short by a leg injury.

"When I lost the ability to play baseball, I began dreaming of being the Braves' announcer, and I worked toward that the rest of my life," said the burly, 47-year-old Bowers, who holds a college degree in speech and communication and is a veteran radio announcer.

His dream came true less than two months before Turner Field's opening when he was informed he'd been chosen from over 350 applicants, only 10 of whom made it to a final live audition. At the time Bowers got the position with the Braves, he was working in Americus, Georgia, where he recorded radio and TV commercials and also served as the P.A. voice for Georgia Southwestern University sports events.

Besides reading the starting lineups and introducing the players at Turner Field, Bowers makes an abundance of varied announcements during a typical game. He usually arrives three hours before game time to begin reviewing a script he said can be as long as 110 pages.

"I love baseball, the tradition of baseball, and talking about baseball," Bowers said. "I've had the opportunity to be at Jacobs Field, Camden Yards and Coors Field, and because of all the things the Braves do for the fans here, I consider Turner Field the modern day field of dreams. I say that because I'm fan-oriented, and I've never seen another ballpark where the fans have so much to do.

"I've got the best seat in the house," said Bowers, who works in the press box and sits above the 'B' in the 'Home of the Braves' sign. "It's a privilege to sit there."

THE CRUSADES

They come by the hundreds, on every day except Monday. They come with uncommon zeal and devotion. And they come hoping to appease an insatiable curiosity, borne of their undying obsession for a shared passion.

They come just as others come to Graceland . . . to the Grand Canyon . . . or even to holy land.

They come to their mecca: Turner Field, Home of the Braves.

They hope to touch history, to see celebrity, to go

Tours include a visit to the Braves clubhouse when the team is on the road or it's the off-season.

Turner Field parking lots are filled with cars from throughout the South.

where only the gifted and privileged tread. And a tour of Turner Field often allows them to do these things and more.

Touch the grass?

Well . . . no.

But, see Chipper Jones' locker? Get Pedro Borbon's autograph? Pick up stray notes from the press box? Sit in the Braves' dugout? Check out the players' renowned putting green? Touch Don Sutton's jacket?

Yes! Yes! All, yes!

The behind-the-scenes tours of Turner Field began May 15 in the ballpark's inaugural season, and the response was so positive that the schedule was soon expanded. By early September, some 13,000 people had taken the tour conducted by the Atlanta History Center.

"The interest is far beyond our expectations," said Carolyn Koch, director of the Ivan Allen Jr. Braves Museum and Hall of Fame where the tours begin. "We get individuals and groups from just about everywhere in the United States and other countries . . . Holland, Germany, Japan.

"Some people just can't leave Atlanta without seeing it. I had one lady from out of town who had her son with her and begged me to let them go on a sold-out tour because her flight left in an hour and a half. I told her the tour lasted an hour, but she insisted on going anyway. I let her, but I don't think she made her flight."

When the Braves are home, tours run from 9:30 a.m.-noon, Tuesday-Saturday. There are no Sunday tours if a home game is scheduled, and no Monday tours, regardless of the team's schedule. When the team is out of town and during the off-season, the tour schedule is 9:30 a.m.-4 p.m., Tuesday-Saturday and 1-4 p.m. Sunday. During the off-season, a special two-hour educational program for school groups enables students to take the regular tour and also learn baseball-based lessons in history, geography, math and physics. Proceeds go to the non-profit Atlanta History Center to maintain and upgrade the museum.

The eyes of children and adults light up when they see all the features that make Turner Field the rarest of diamonds, but, naturally, their excitement reaches a peak when they visit the Braves' clubhouse (only when the team is out of town) and dugout. The press box and broadcast booth are close behind, though.

"People are just fascinated by the Braves' clubhouse and the putting green," said Koch. "And when they get to the dugout, it's just, 'Wow!' One of the biggest things they want to do is touch the grass.

Nathan Reich (center) enjoys his 10th birthday with brother Emerson (r) and friends Andy (l) and Whitney Sharpe.

MARK REICH

They're constantly asking to do it. So we have to have trailers who watch and make sure they don't touch it.

"In the press box, people like to pick up any left-over game notes or scraps of paper they see. They love it when they find notes the announcers have left in the broadcast booth. And Don Sutton's TBS jacket that he wears to do the introduction for games is hanging there. They like to touch that, and some of them stick notes in it."

Though the tours are scripted, and thus rather predictable, occasionally there's a surprise.

"One day a tour was extremely late getting back," Koch said. "When they finally came in, we asked what had taken so long. They said (injured relief pitcher) Pedro Borbon showed up in the clubhouse and signed autographs for everyone. It was quite a treat for them."

Though such an autograph adventure is rare indeed, a tour of Turner Field still provides fans a unique perspective on the new Home of the Braves and furnishes them with an experience few will ever forget.

A FAN'S VIEW

Mark Reich is a 38-year-old engineer who lives with his wife and two sons in Burlington, North Carolina, some 350 miles northeast of Atlanta. He's been watching Braves games on TBS longer than he can remember but didn't see one in person until 1991. Since then, the 12-hour roundtrip drive to Atlanta has become an annual pilgrimage.

In early May, Reich gave his youngest son, Nathan, a much-anticipated present for his 10th birthday — a trip to see the Braves at Turner Field. It turned into the kind of weekend that stays with a youngster the rest of his life.

The Reichs, Mark and wife Janie, Nathan and 13-year-old Emerson, were accompanied by their friends, Dickie and Debbie Sharpe and their children, Andy (14) and Whitney (11).

"We left early Friday morning, and we got to Turner Field in time to walk around before batting practice, then we watched batting practice," Reich said. "We were in the club level in right field the first night. Having the TV monitors made it real nice. The next night we were in the upper deck right behind home plate, and those were really good seats.

"It's a wonderful place to watch a game. They did an excellent job laying it out. It's layed out for baseball. The boys had a great time. The food was outstanding. Even though the Braves lost, it was exciting baseball. We took a lot of pictures in Monument Grove. We got there both nights when the gates opened. The boys played the games in Scout's Alley and went to the museum. We didn't get to see everything, but what we saw was fantastic.

"We spent a lot of time in the outfield watching them take batting practice and infield, and on Saturday night, we caught a home run ball Ryan Klesko hit in batting practice.

"But the highlight was after the game Saturday. Nathan wanted to get some autographs, so he and I went around to the back gate and waited for the players to come out. Mike Mordecai stopped and signed a ball. And Nathan is persistent. He didn't want to leave until all the cars were gone.

"After a while, there were only three cars left. Bobby Cox came out and signed a ball. There were only three or four fans left, then John Smoltz came out and signed a ball for Nathan. That just thrilled him to death.

"The kids really enjoyed Turner Field. It's just a great facility to watch baseball. I wish everyone could see it."

Denny Neagle was 10-1 at Turner Field en route to being the National League's only 20-game winner in 1997.

THE FIRST SEASON

When you move into a new house, you're tentative, unsure of yourself. Does that door lead to the bathroom or is it a closet? Where's the switch for this light? And where are the cereal bowls?

After a while, you settle in, and everything becomes second nature. Slowly but surely, the house becomes your home.

Apparently, no one bothered to inform the Braves about experiencing a get-acquainted period at Turner Field. Because they didn't need one.

Bobby Cox's team took to its new home like Andruw Jones took to playing in the '96 World Series at age 19. Home run! Home run!

In the Braves' case, it was win, win, win, and win some more. After an uninspiring (10-18) spring training and losing two of three games at Houston to open the season, Atlanta christened Turner Field by winning the first five games played there and 12 of the first 13 en route to a major league record 19-victory April.

"Thanks for the memories, Atlanta-Fulton County Stadium, but this move across the street suits us just fine!"

The impressive start was a tribute to the professionalism the team has exhibited throughout the '90s. Many clubs — no matter how talented — might have come unglued if they encountered the circumstances the Braves faced to open the season.

On March 25, just a week before Opening Day, John Schuerholz sent shock waves through all of baseball — particularly the Braves' clubhouse and fan base — by trading two-thirds of his starting outfield. He sent 1995 World Series hero David Justice and hometown star Marquis Grissom to Cleveland for five-time American League stolen

Kenny Lofton brought a refreshing burst of speed to Turner Field.

base champ Kenny Lofton and left-handed reliever Alan Embree.

Two days later, before that deal had been fully digested, Schuerholz struck again. This time, he sent popular young outfielder Jermaine Dye and reliever Jamie Walker to Kansas City for left-handed-hitting outfielder Michael Tucker and reserve infielder Keith Lockhart.

Both trades received mixed reviews.

Justice and Grissom, All-Star performers, were immensely popular with Braves fans, while Lofton was in the final year of his contract and could walk away from Atlanta as a free agent at the end of the season.

Dye filled in admirably when Justice was injured in '96 and seemed to have a promising future in Atlanta, while Tucker and Lockhart were unknown factors to fans and the media — though not to the Braves.

The final week of spring training was a whirlwind, and not just because of the trades. On March 26, the day between the two deals, the Braves said goodbye to their West Palm Beach spring training facility that had been their Florida base since 1963.

Two days later, they played the first game at the new Disney Wide World of Sports Complex in Lake Buena Vista, Florida, that will become their spring training home in 1998. And from there, the Braves headed directly to Atlanta for a dress rehearsal at Turner Field in the form of two exhibition games against the Yankees (for the record, a 2-0 win March 29, followed by a 5-3 loss).

Michael Tucker (l) played some sweet music at the new ballpark, and Jeff Blauser got the rhythm back in his game, too.

TOMMY BUTLER

Greg and Kathy Maddux introduced their children to Turner Field on Family Day.

Two ballpark christenings within 24 hours, whew, then off to Houston for the April 1 season opener. It's no wonder the Braves didn't play quite like defending National League champs against the Astros, in spite of getting strong pitching from John Smoltz, the '96 National League Cy Young Award winner, in the opener (a 2-1 loss) and Greg Maddux, the '95 Cy recipient, in the second game (4-3).

As a tuneup for the inaugural regular season game at Turner Field, the Braves wrapped up the series at the Astrodome with a 3-2 win behind Tom Glavine's pitching and a home run by Fred McGriff.

Back in Atlanta, the Cubs arrived with hopes of spoiling the stirring Turner Field festivities befitting the baptism of baseball's newest temple. And for most of the evening, it looked as if they might do just that — until a two-run rally in the eighth produced a 5-4 Braves victory.

Yes, eight innings is all it took for the Braves to feel comfortable at Turner Field. They swept three from the Cubs, then took the first two from Houston for five straight wins at 755 Hank Aaron Drive and six overall. In the first game against the Astros, Jeff Blauser was 4-for-4 to give him eight consecutive hits, just two shy of the NL record. And in the second Houston game, Fred McGriff walked with the bases loaded in the 12th inning (the first extra-inning game at the park, if you're keeping score) to plate the decisive run.

The Braves' first loss at "The Ted" finally came on April 10, a 5-3 setback to the Astros. But after a weekend road trip to frigid Chicago, the team returned home and swept three games from Cincinnati in dominating fashion. Atlanta pounded 19 hits en route to a 15-5 whipping of the Reds in the series opener. The next night, pitching was the story — John Smoltz authoring the first complete game shutout at Turner Field (3-0). And in the series finale, Blauser and Lofton homered for a 7-1 decision.

It seemed everything was working. As usual, there was excellent pitching, timely hitting and solid defense. But what everyone wanted to talk about was speed — a relatively rare commodity on Braves teams. The presence of Lofton at the top of the order and Tucker hitting right behind him gave the Braves a surprisingly swift tandem that revved the offense, rattled opponents, and tightened the defense. The new additions appeared to bring out aggressive baserunning in some of the other players, and by the end of April, the team actually had more stolen bases than home runs.

Other April highlights at Turner Field included:

▮ Andruw Jones' two-run, 10th-inning home run April 26 (three days after his 20th birthday) to beat San Diego, 3-2.

▮ Maddux beating the Padres, 2-0, in 1 hour, 16 minutes on April 27 in a game called after four and a half innings due to rain.

▮ An 18-hit, 14-0 blistering of the Dodgers on April 28 that made Glavine 4-0 and the NL Pitcher of the Month.

The Braves finished the month 19-6 (.760) and led the league in both team batting average (.317) and staff ERA (2.56). At Turner Field, they were 12-2 (.857). Home, sweet home!

But in early May, the National League discovered that the Braves were not invincible in their new surroundings. In fact, Cox's team displayed some sluggishness early in the month in spite of Blauser's torrid hitting and the usual fine work from the starting pitchers. By losing two of three to the budget-conscious Pirates and losing both games of a two-game set with Florida — all at Turner Field — Atlanta allowed the social-climbing Marlins to pull within three games of the division lead.

Of more concern, though, were serious threats to the health of Maddux and Glavine. On May 2, Maddux not only had a string of 32 consecutive scoreless innings broken by Pittsburgh, but he also was hit on the right arm by a line drive by the Pirates' Kevin Elster.

Maddux was able to stay in the game and didn't miss a start, but that wasn't the case with Glavine, who was hit on the left hand by an inside pitch while trying to bunt against Florida's Tony Saunders May 8. The Braves feared their ace lefthander had a broken bone, but the injury wasn't nearly that serious, allowing Glavine to return to the rotation after missing just one turn.

The Braves' lethargic 7-7 May start carried into their May 16 game against St. Louis at Turner Field. In fact, the Cardinals' Alan Benes had them in such a deep funk that night that he nearly put his name on what would have been the most-coveted of Turner Field "firsts" — a no-hitter. But with two outs in the ninth inning of a scoreless game, Tucker's double ended Benes' bid for a place in history. And with nothing but zeros still on the scoreboard in the bottom of the 13th, Andruw Jones' checked-swing infield hit with two outs produced the only run in a memorable, if not picturesque, Atlanta victory.

Perhaps inspired by narrowly averting the embarrassment of a no-hitter, the Braves proceeded to blitz through the last six games of the homestand by winning all four from St. Louis and two from Montreal.

ALLISON SHIRREFFS

Greg Maddux had another masterful season in 1997 and signed on for five more years as a Brave.

MAPPING THE FUTURE

Some of the biggest news in Turner Field's inaugural season was made behind the scenes rather than on the field. By signing Greg Maddux and Tom Glavine to long-term contracts, the Braves demonstrated their commitment to providing championship baseball at their new ballpark through the end of the millennium and beyond.

With Glavine and Maddux in the last year of their contracts, the Braves broke with tradition and signed both in the midst of the '97 season, thus eliminating the possibility of losing them via free agency.

On May 22 in a press conference at Turner Field, Stan Kasten and John Schuerholz announced an agreement with Glavine, the '91 Cy Young Award winner, on a four-year contract worth $34 million with an option for a fifth year at $9 million. Then in a similar scene on Aug. 10, the Braves revealed a five-year, $57.5-million deal with Maddux that likely will make the four-time Cy Young Award winner the highest-paid player in the game in '98.

With '96 Cy Young winner John Smoltz and Denny Neagle already under contract at least through 2000, the Team of the '90s guaranteed itself a most-formidable starting rotation into the next century.

"I hope to help this team win a couple of more World Championships the next four or five years. There's nothing like that feeling we got in 1995," said Glavine, who pitched one of the greatest games in Braves — and baseball — history when he beat Cleveland, 1-0, in decisive Game 6 of the 1995 World Series.

"We (Braves players) talk all the time about how fortunate we are to play here," said the 31-year-old lefthander. "No one wanted to play here in the late '80s, but now everyone wants to play here. The total commitment to winning is there, and guys who have been with us and are now with other teams tell us all the time, 'You don't know how good you've got it.'"

What's the future hold for Turner Field? No one knows for sure, but by signing Maddux and Glavine, the Braves eliminated any doubt about their intentions for continued rule of the National League.

Cal Ripken Jr. found his signature was in big demand at Turner Field.

THE HIGHLIGHTS:

▮ Lofton's third 5-hit game of the season — one shy of the major league record — to pace a 19-hit, 11-6 pasting of the Cardinals May 18.

▮ Denny Neagle raising his record to 7-0 with a 7-3 win in the series finale against St. Louis that featured a potential game-saving, headlong, diving catch in right by Tucker that will be featured on Braves highlight videos for a long time. It concluded the club's first four-game sweep at home since July 1991.

▮ And, finally, a game-ending, two-run, pinch-hit home run by Lockhart with one out in the ninth on May 21 that turned a near 2-1 loss to Montreal into a 3-2 victory.

Those heroics made the Braves 19-6 at Turner Field — a cool .760 — through nearly one-third of their home dates.

After winning three of five games on a quick swing to the West coast, the Braves returned home for more Turner Field heroics from Tucker, who perhaps more than any of his teammates, had established 755 Hank Aaron Drive as his personal playground during the first two months of the season.

An absence of clutch hitting plagued Atlanta during a loss to the Giants in opening the final homestand of May. More of the same had them locked in a 2-2, ninth-inning tie with San Francisco May 30. But with one out, Lofton drew a walk and stole second. Tucker followed with a single to right, allowing Lofton to scoot home and sending a happy crowd to the parking lots.

Yet the Braves could win only one of the last four games of the homestand. They split four with San Francisco and dropped two to San Diego. That was primarily the consequence of .141 hitting with runners in scoring position and resulted in a 2-4 stay. It wasn't exactly the ideal way to go into a brutal stretch of 24 of 31 games on the road leading into the All-Star break, but it would have to do.

The next three home dates didn't fall until the middle of June, and though they brought a World Series-like atmosphere to Turner Field, the results were less than encouraging. The Baltimore Orioles, owners of the best record in the American League, visited Atlanta for the first interleague series in Braves history. Three sellouts that included hordes of Orioles fans watched as Cal Ripken Jr. extended his consecutive games played streak to 2,380 while Baltimore pulled off the first three-game sweep of the home team in Turner Field history.

After another week and a half on the road, the Braves came home to finish the month against some welcome visitors — the moribund Phillies. Cox's team proceeded to wipe out any lingering memories of recent Turner Field struggles (just two wins in their last nine home dates) by sweeping four from Philadelphia.

The pitching of Neagle and Maddux highlighted the first two games of the series. A pair of home runs by Tucker — a Turner Field first — thrilled the ballpark's largest crowd to date (48,557) for the third game in which both teams wore replica 1938 Negro Leagues uniforms to commemorate the 50th anniversary of Jackie Robinson breaking the color barrier in the majors.

The big bang of the series was saved for last, though, and was delivered courtesy of Lockhart.

With Atlanta trailing, 5-1, in the sixth, the utility-man came off the bench with the bases loaded to produce a rarity and yet another Turner Field first — a pinch-hit grand slam. That tied the score and the Braves went on to win, 6-5, giving them a 25-13 record (.658) at home prior to the All-Star break.

Following the All-Star Game in Cleveland, where Cox took seven of his players (Blauser, Glavine, Chipper Jones, Lofton, Javy Lopez, Maddux and Neagle), the Braves continued their grand slam observation of Turner Field's inaugural season.

On July 10, the first game after the break, Chipper Jones hit his third bases-loaded home run in a span of just 13 games. It made him the first Atlanta Brave to hit three slams in the same season, but unfortunately, it was wasted in a 10-7 loss to the Mets. It was the Braves' sixth grand slam of the season, but their slam-a-thon was just warming up.

Four nights later, catcher Tim Spehr, just called up from Richmond, and Ryan Klesko hit grand slams in consecutive innings to spur a 10-6 victory against Philadelphia. The double shot gave the Braves six grand slams in six weeks and eight for the season, tying the franchise record.

Nevertheless, all was not good for Cox's team as the second half got underway. Even with a 12-game homestand — the longest of the season — awaiting them, the Braves struggled. They dropped three of four to the Mets and went only 6-6 before massive Turner Field crowds. The stand closed with four consecutive sellouts against the Dodgers that produced a franchise-record attendance of 196,211 for a four-game series but a 2-2 split on the field. A then-Turner Field record of 49,758 fans attended the July 19 game, and the inaugural season sellout tally reached 18 — double the number in all of '96.

In the midst of the homestand, though,

Andruw Jones shows his 1938 replica Atlanta Black Crackers jersey to Negro Leagues legend Buck O'Neill.

FOUNTAINE LEWIS

Rookies (l-r) Mike Cather, Chad Fox and Kevin Millwood gave the pitching staff a mid-season facelift.

Schuerholz saw fit to give the team — especially the bullpen — a wakeup call. He sent relievers Joe Borowski, Paul Byrd and Brad Clontz to Richmond in one fell swoop and replaced them with three rookies — Mike Cather, Chad Fox and Kevin Millwood — who didn't have an inning of big league experience among them.

The newcomers performed surprisingly well, yet the 6-6 homestand still left the Braves 20-18 at Turner Field since they christened the ballpark by winning 12 of their first 13.

After a short roadtrip, the Braves closed the home portion of their July schedule by sweeping three games from the meek Cubs. Neagle raised his record to 14-2 with a shutout in the first game of the series; Andruw Jones had a home run and two other hits, stole a base, and made two excellent catches to highlight the second game; and reserve outfielder Danny Bautista delivered a triple to key a two-run, ninth-inning rally in the finale. It was a nice way to head into August and the final third of the season.

Through most of the first two-thirds of the season, there was little talk of a pennant race. However, that changed when the Braves went to Florida and dropped three of four to the second-place Marlins in the first of two four-game series with their nearest competition in a 12-game span. When Cox's team returned to Turner Field to start an eight-game homestand August 6, the lead over Florida was just 4 1/2 games.

That was in jeopardy of slipping to 3 1/2 in the first game of the homestand against the Cardinals. But with the game tied, 3-3, Bautista came through again, this time with a game-ending pinch-hit home run to lead off the ninth. The next night, Neagle raised his record to 16-2 and ran his consecutive scoreless innings streak to 23 2/3 by beating St. Louis, 3-0. More importantly, the victory enabled the Braves to pad their lead to 5 1/2 games as the Marlins came calling.

In front of yet another standing-room-only crowd at Turner Field, Florida opened the series with a 6-4 victory. It was the Marlins' seventh win in nine games against the Braves and had the faithful getting a little edgy. On Saturday afternoon, Smoltz got the Atlanta lead back to 5 1/2 games with a 4-3 victory.

The Marlins won the third game, 4-2, in 10 innings, but in the end, they left town as they arrived — 5 1/2 games in arrears. That's because the Braves salvaged a split of the series with a 2-1 victory in the Monday finale, courtesy of an unheralded player who'd suddenly become a familiar hero. With the bases loaded and one out in a 1-1 game, Bautista — a minor leaguer for most of the season — delivered a pinch-hit sacrifice fly. It was his second game-ending swing off the bench in just six days.

But the split with the Marlins only served to temporarily conceal the Braves' worst offensive slump of the season. Pittsburgh, playing under .500, came to Turner Field next and promptly swept a two-game

series. In the first game, Neagle turned over a 2-1 lead to Mark Wohlers in the ninth inning, and the Pirates proceeded to score four times for a 5-2 victory. The next night, Smoltz worked nine strong innings, only to lose, 2-1. A Florida victory pulled the Marlins within 4 1/2 again.

August was nearly half over, and the Braves were hitting an alarming .210 for the month. A five-game road trip did little to revitalize the offense, but the bats showed some signs of life upon returning to Turner Field for three games against Cincinnati August 22-24. Maddux was roughed up but still won the first game, 6-2. Then in the second game, the Braves had their biggest uprising in nearly a month and a half, winning 10-3 as Neagle matched Maddux with his 17th victory. Prosperity was short-lived, though, because the Reds won the finale, 6-4, when the Braves committed three errors that led to four unearned runs in the last three innings.

Cox's team bounced back to take two of three from Central division leader Houston, yet the loss in the middle game kept people questioning what was wrong with the Braves. Maddux turned a 3-1 lead over to Wohlers in the ninth, but the Astros promptly tied the game, then won it in the 13th.

After a robust three-game whipping of the Red Sox at Boston's historic Fenway Park, the Braves returned home seemingly charged for three more interleague games against the young Detroit Tigers. But it was the visitors who took two out of three. The Braves' lone victory came in the middle game, a 5-0 win in which Neagle pitched his fourth shutout of the season to go 19-3 and hit the first home run of the season by an Atlanta pitcher.

With but a 3 1/2-game division lead, the Braves left for six games on the West coast. They still held a fine 43-27 record at Turner Field — but only 31-26 at home since the 12-1 start.

The Joneses, Andruw (l) and Chipper, bask in the nostalgia of Boston's Fenway Park.

The division race seemed to be under control after the Braves won five of six at San Diego and Los Angeles to increase their lead over Florida to 6 1/2 games. But three days after returning to Turner Field for the final homestand of the season, the margin had dropped to 4 1/2 due to a sweep at the hands of the inspired Rockies.

The first Colorado game, prior to which the Braves welcomed the 3-millionth fan to Turner Field, was the toughest to take. Maddux handed a 1-0 lead to Wohlers after eight innings, and moments later, the Rockies were 3-1 winners.

Some teams might panic in such circumstances. Indeed, there was a great deal of apprehension about the Braves' play at Turner Field — 18-17 since the All-Star break — and the club's overall inconsistencies. However, all Cox's tested and proven team did was knuckle down and reel off six straight victories against the Giants, Mets and Expos. In the process, the Braves clinched a playoff berth, closed on their sixth straight division title, and had a grand-slamming good time doing it.

The sweep at the hands of the Rockies still seemed to be on the Braves' minds when they opened a two-game set with the Giants September 15. They entered the ninth inning trailing, 4-1, when suddenly, fortunes were reversed. Three singles and an infield grounder made it 4-3, then McGriff sent the Turner Field crowd dancing to their cars with a game-ending, two-run home run.

The next night, backup catcher Eddie Perez, of all players, etched his name and the Braves' in the

Fred McGriff's home run capped a memorable, game-winning rally against San Francisco on September 15.

record book with a grand slam that highlighted a 6-4 victory over the Giants. It was the Braves' 11th grand slam of the season, tying the major league record. A share of the record wasn't enough, though. The very next night, Klesko hit the Braves' 12th bases-loaded home run of the season in the midst of a 9-run first inning against the Mets.

Just like that, any phobia the Braves and their fans had about playing at Turner Field was long forgotten, as were the pesky Fish from south Florida. That win assured Atlanta a playoff spot and left the Marlins six games in arrears with just a week and a half to go.

Appropriately, the division clinching came on September 22, the last home date of the regular season. After three weekend sellouts against Montreal that brought the inaugural season total to 33, the Braves beat the Expos, 3-2, before a Monday night crowd of 41,268 to wrap up a record sixth consecutive division title and bring total attendance to 3,463,988 — second in franchise history and nearly a 20 percent increase over '96.

Actually, Cox's team and the crowd found out during the game that Florida lost, mathematically eliminating the second-place Marlins. But for good measure, the Braves dispatched Montreal in most unusual fashion, Bautista scoring the winning run in the bottom of the 11th inning when Mike Mordecai struck out on Steve Kline's wild pitch with one out and the bases loaded.

Since the advent of division play in 1969, it was the first time a team had won six consecutive titles. And so, it was on to the post-season. Turner Field had been christened in style.

Knucksie's Night

Perhaps no other player in history has spoken so openly and so frequently about the joy he received

from his career with the Braves as has Phil Niekro. So, it was fitting that on the evening of September 17 at Turner Field, the Braves returned the favor by honoring their legendary knuckleball pitcher for his latest and greatest accomplishment — enshrinement in the National Baseball Hall of Fame at Cooperstown, New York.

To the delight of a crowd of some 41,000, a highlights video of Niekro's career was shown, all-time home run king Hank Aaron was among those who paid tribute to him, and Braves president Stan Kasten and general manager John Schuerholz presented him with a custom glass sculpture commemorating his induction.

"He represents what's good about baseball," said Braves chairman Bill Bartholomay.

During the pre-game ceremony, Niekro also was given a giant congratulatory greeting card that was signed in the ballpark's plaza by hundreds of fans.

"There are a lot of trophies in my trophy case. The one I cherish most is the cap with the 'A' on it for Atlanta Braves," said Niekro, who was elected to the Hall of Fame in January 1997 and inducted August 3 of Turner Field's inaugural season.

Niekro has never made a secret of his love for the Braves. The plaque on his statue outside Turner Field reads: "There's no better Braves fan anywhere than I." That's a sentiment he's expressed countless times.

At the Atlanta-Fulton County news conference after he was notified of his election, Niekro said, "Playing for the Braves and Ted Turner — putting on a Braves cap every day — was the greatest experience a ballplayer can have."

And in his induction speech at Cooperstown, Niekro said, "They (Braves) are absolutely, to me, the first-class organization in the country."

Knucksie, the feeling is mutual.

There's nothing like a new Hall of Famer to help break in a new ballpark.

TOMMY BUTLER

ALLISON SHIRRIEFFS

ALL DRESSED UP

There's nothing quite like bunting to dress up a ballpark. Its "black tie," baseball style. It signifies the most special time — the post-season.

Turner Field never looked anything less than immaculate throughout its Inaugural Season, but come September 30, it was even more exquisite than usual. All decked out in bunting, basking in brilliant sunshine, and refreshed by a nice breeze, the new Home of the Braves looked positively dazzling for its first really big show.

Fortunately, the home team looked just as smart as its quarters.

The underdog Houston Astros, winners of the National League Central Division, hoped to spoil the Division Series party for the defending National League champions. But the Braves would have none of that nonsense.

With cool efficiency, Atlanta won the first two games at Turner Field, then completed a sweep in the best-of-five series by eliminating Houston in Game 3 at the Astrodome.

It didn't take long for the high drama of the post-season to permeate the grounds at 755 Hank Aaron Drive in the Division Series opener. The Braves turned a leadoff bloop double by Kenny Lofton in the first inning into a run and got a leadoff home run by Ryan Klesko in the second to take a quick 2-0 lead behind Greg Maddux. Those were the only

ALLISON SHIRREFFS

Glavine won Game Two against the Astros.

two hits — and runs — the offense produced, but Maddux made the lead stand, yielding only a run in the fifth. Tension filled the air with two outs in the eighth when Houston strongman Jeff Bagwell worked the count to 3-2, only to strike out on a Maddux changeup, stranding the potential tying run at second and bringing the faithful to their feet with a thundering roar.

"Two hits, two runs . . . its a funny game," Bobby Cox said.

In many ways, Game 1 set the tone for what would prove to be a "funny," though certainly not humorous, '97 post-season.

The drama of Game 2 quickly evaporated in the fifth inning when a two-run, pinch-hit single by

Greg Colbrunn broke open a game the Braves eventually won, 13-3.

Tom Glavine was uncharacteristically erratic in the early innings, allowing the Astros to tie the game, 3-3, in the fourth after Jeff Blauser's three-run home run in the third gave the Turner Field crowd room to relax.

Then in the fifth, the Braves pushed across one run and had the bases loaded when Cox sent up Colbrunn to bat for Klesko. He bounced a single to right, making it 6-3, and the rout was on. After Glavine got out of a jam in the sixth, thanks to a leaping catch against the stands by Andruw Jones of a Craig Biggio foul ball, the Braves scored five more in the bottom of the inning to put it out of reach.

It was on to Houston for Game 3, but no one felt more at home in the Astrodome than John Smoltz. The Atlanta righthander completely dominated the Astros, striking out 11 and limiting them to three hits and one walk in a 4-1 victory. It was Smoltz's 10th post-season win, tying him with Whitey Ford and Dave Stewart for the all-time record.

Just like that, the Braves eliminated Houston, 1-2-3, and headed back to Turner Field to host the Florida Marlins for the opening of the National League Championship Series October 7.

With the defense of the pennant at stake, the Braves played like anything but National League champions in Game 1 of the NLCS. A two-out, first-inning error by Fred McGriff and a groundball double by Moises Alou down the third-base line that Chipper Jones thought he should have fielded resulted in a quick 3-0 lead for the Marlins. An error in the third by Lofton resulted in two more runs for the visitors. Though the Braves fought back with home runs by Chipper Jones and Klesko, the 5-3 final saddled Maddux with a defeat in which he didn't allow a single earned run.

The Braves gave away the home-field advantage in Game 1, but they restored some order at Turner Field in Game 2. Thanks to a splendid outing by Glavine and a two-run home run by Klesko in the first inning, they jumped to a 3-0 lead and cruised to a 7-1 victory.

"I'm not going to say this wasn't a big game," said Glavine, who retired the first nine men he faced and had a two-hit shutout until Devon White delivered an RBI-double with one out in the eighth. "We didn't want to go to Florida down two games."

The three games in Miami were much like the first two in Atlanta — a mixed bag for the Braves. Charles Johnson's three-run double in the sixth inning did in Smoltz and was the difference in the Marlins' 5-2 victory in Game 3. However, a masterful, four-hit complete game by Denny Neagle produced a 4-0 victory in Game 4, evening the series and guaranteeing more baseball for Turner Field's Inaugural Season.

Though the Braves were able to return home, they did so with their backs against the wall. That was because Florida won Game 5, 2-1, amid considerable controversy created by the wide strike zone afforded Marlins rookie pitcher Livan Hernandez by umpire Eric Gregg.

The Braves and their fans were well aware that the team overcame a 3-1 deficit in games to win the '96 NLCS against St. Louis, so they knew winning two straight "must" games was not out of the question. A record Turner Field crowd of 50,446, armed with complimentary red foam tomahawks, set a new standard for chopping, chanting and just plain screaming at the new ballpark in Game 6. Nevertheless, the Braves were stopped short of a fifth World Series in the '90s by a 7-4 setback.

Florida scored four times in the first inning against Glavine and got their other three runs in the sixth. Spurred by four hits from second baseman

ALLISON SHIRREFFS

Keith Lockhart's bat was a post-season surprise.

Keith Lockhart, the Braves fought back throughout the evening . . . and down to the last out — a grounder to second by Chipper Jones who represented the potential tying run. But it was the upstart Marlins, born in 1993, who advanced to the Series and did so in record time for an expansion team.

"We gave it everything we had. It just wasn't enough," said Cox. "I'm very proud of this ballclub. It was another great year. Every city would be happy to have six division titles in a row, and I'm sure this city is."

Indeed. While the proceedings ended a little sooner than the Braves and their fans would have liked, it still was an extraordinary Inaugural Season for Turner Field, rarest of diamonds.

Atlanta-Fulton County Stadium is nothing but a memory now — but what a memory!

BRAVES HOMES IN HISTORY

It was the stadium that introduced major league sports to the South. For years, it was commonly known as The Launching Pad, much to the dismay of pitchers everywhere. It was the ballpark Pascual Perez got lost trying to find and that Chief Noc-a-Homa called home. It's where Pete Rose's 44-game hitting streak ended in 1978 and the miracle of 1991 unfolded. And most of all, it's the house where Hank caught the Babe and the '95 Braves won Atlanta's first World Championship.

Atlanta Stadium, which became Atlanta-Fulton County Stadium in 1976, was the site of some of the most thrilling and momentous events in Braves and baseball history. It was often characterized by horrendous baseball and a sea of empty seats. But in its last six seasons, it was mobbed by frenzied, tomahawk-chopping hordes wallowing in one of the most prosperous periods in franchise history.

Then, following the 1996 season, it was put out to pasture as the Braves prepared to move across the street into Turner Field. To many fans, Atlanta-Fulton County Stadium was hallowed ground. The thrills of 1991-96, in particular, guarantee it will always be remembered fondly by thousands of fans throughout the Southeast who made annual pilgrimages there and by thousands more across the nation who watched its history unfold on the TBS Superstation.

Many Braves followers, especially the younger version and the relatively new converts, aren't aware that

Atlanta-Fulton County Stadium is just one of six previous home parks the franchise has played in since it was founded in 1871. Four of those were "permanent" residences and two were just temporary quarters.

The South End Grounds and Braves Field were the two long-term homes in the club's Boston era from 1871-1952. But Fenway Park and the Congress Street Grounds also housed it on a temporary basis in Boston. The team moved to Wisconsin and into Milwaukee County Stadium in 1953 before relocating to the South in 1966.

SOUTH END GROUNDS

The South End Grounds served as the franchise's home for most of its first 44 seasons, the longest it stayed in any of its four long-term ballparks.

It had the only double-decked grandstand of the ballparks that have been used over the years by Boston's major league baseball teams. Its most distinctive architectural feature were the spires atop the grandstand.

The dimensions of the 11,000-seat South End Grounds were 250 feet down the left-field line, 255 down the right-field line, and 440 feet to the center-field fence.

There were 50-cent bleachers running down the first-base line, and it was under these bleachers where the fire started that destroyed the original

The South End Grounds was the Braves' first home ballpark.

grandstand on May 15, 1894. The blaze erupted in the third inning, though reports differ as to its cause. Some claimed it was set by boys burning trash underneath the seats. Others said it was set off by a lighted cigar falling into peanut shells.

The flames spread quickly, and the game was called in a 3-3 tie. The fire destroyed everything — the bleachers, the grandstand, and an estimated 170 buildings, including a school and a fire station, covering 12 acres around the park. The 1893 pennant also went up in flames. Estimates of the total damage were as high as $1 million, and some 1,000 people were left homeless.

Over the next two months, some of the team's home games were played on the road, but most were played at the Congress Street Grounds. By July 20, the park had been rebuilt and the Beaneaters, as the Braves were then known, returned.

Few ballparks have ever witnessed as much success as the South End Grounds. In 44 seasons there, the Red Stockings, who became the Beaneaters in 1883 (and the Braves in 1912), won 13 league champi-

onships and one World Series. The club won the last four National Association titles in 1872-75, then won nine National League pennants there (1877-78, 1883, 1891-93, 1897-98 and 1914).

CONGRESS STREET GROUNDS

The Congress Street Grounds offered only a temporary address for the franchise, but it provided the site for one of the greatest offensive displays in baseball history.

When the South End Grounds burned, the best available ballpark where the team could play its home games was this small wooden structure with a 250-foot left-field fence located adjacent to Boston Harbor.

Just two weeks after the fire, Boston second baseman Bobby Lowe took advantage of the short target in left to become the first player to hit four home runs in the same game. Only 11 other players — two of them Braves — have duplicated the feat.

Since many early ballparks were built with railroads and highways beyond the outfield fences, legends unfolded of "long distance" home runs landing on a freight car or truck and being carried across the country. But lore has it that the "longest" homer of all was hit at the Congress Street Grounds. The ball landed on an Australia-bound ship in Boston Harbor and traveled halfway around the world!

FENWAY PARK

The name Fenway Park is pure magic to most baseball fans. The ancient home of the Boston Red Sox with its famous Green Monster left-field wall is one of the last of the nostalgic urban ballparks and invokes memories of Ted Williams, Carl Yastrzemski, and Carlton Fisk waving his home run fair in the fabulous 1975 World Series.

But Fenway should have additional sentimental meaning to Braves fans, for not only did it once serve as the team's home, albeit on a temporary basis, but it also was the site of one of the greatest triumphs in franchise history. It was at Fenway that the so-called "Miracle" Braves of 1914 completed their astounding World Series sweep of the highly favored Philadelphia Athletics.

On April 12, 1912, Fenway Park opened as Boston's new home for the Red Sox of the American League. The Braves first played at Fenway in 1913, when the Red Sox allowed them to use it for the Memorial Day doubleheader to accommodate large crowds.

During the last month of the 1914 season, the Braves also used Fenway when the South End Grounds couldn't handle the crowds eager to see the club pull off one of the most improbable of all league championships by climbing from last place on July 18. Games 3 and 4 of the World Series were also played there.

The Braves continued to play some home games at Fenway in 1915 until Braves Field opened on

The Braves revisited Fenway Park this year after a 45-year absence from Boston.

Braves Field was a huge ballpark where home runs were scarce.

August 18. It seemed the Braves would never have to borrow Fenway again. However, they had to return 31 years later, if only for a couple of days.

The seats at Braves Field received a fresh coat of green paint for the 1946 opener. But the paint on some seats had not completely dried when fans arrived. Consequently, many departed with green splotches on their clothes. To make sure there weren't more paint problems, the opening series was finished at Fenway.

BRAVES FIELD

Team owner James Gaffney built Braves Field with the idea that it would be the "perfect ballpark." Obviously, he was a pitchers' owner.

The most distinctive feature of the park the defending World Series champion Braves moved into on August 18, 1915 was the vast expanse of out-

field grass. Just prior to the opening, the great Ty Cobb — the "Georgia Peach" — visited the site when the Tigers were in town to play the Red Sox. Standing at home plate, he surveyed the distant target and remarked, "No home run will ever go over that fence. This is the only field in the country on which you can play an absolutely fair game of ball without the interference of fences."

That's what Gaffney had in mind. He didn't dislike home runs. He just thought they should be of the inside-the-park variety, and he wanted the outfield to be designed so that a homer could be hit to any field without clearing the fence.

When Braves Field opened, the left- and right-field foul lines extended 402 feet from home plate. Straightaway center field was 520 feet, and deepest center — just to the right — was 550 feet.

The outfield distance was changed numerous times in the 37-plus seasons the club played at Braves Field. But until it was significantly shortened in 1928, only seven over-the-fence home runs were hit compared to 209 inside-the-park ones.

It took nearly two years for the first over-the-fence home run and almost a full decade for the first homer to clear the left-field fence.

Capacity was 43,500, but estimates of the total number of fans packed into the park for its opening ranged as high as 56,000. It was easily the largest crowd in baseball history at the time.

Sporting Life noted that Braves Field had the latest in modern conveniences: "Clubhouses are under the grandstand and equipped with showers" and "retiring rooms have been located in the different sections of the field, making it the best laid out plant that has ever been arranged for."

Concessions included a hot pastrami sandwich, fried clams and steamed clams with a little jug of baked beans on the side.

"It is the last word in baseball parks," proclaimed National League president John K. Tener, who helped raise the 1914 pennant at the opening of Braves Field.

MILWAUKEE COUNTY STADIUM

Milwaukee County Stadium was the first major league ballpark financed entirely by public funds and the first big league stadium built with lights included.

Not until March 18, 1953, three days after County Stadium was opened to the public, did Milwaukee learn that the Braves were moving to Wisconsin. Despite no off-season ticket sales, the team that drew a pitiful 281,278 fans to Braves Field in 1952 attracted a then-National League record 1,826,397 to County Stadium in 1953.

When the Braves reached Milwaukee, they found a ballpark much to their liking. Built specifically for baseball, the park's dimensions were 320 feet down both lines, 404 to center and 392 to left- and right-center.

On May 20, in only their 13th home game, the Braves passed their entire 1952 attendance in Boston. Milwaukee was sold on the Braves. County Stadium attendance topped 2 million for the next four years, peaking at 2,215,404 in the

Milwaukee County Stadium was home to the great Braves teams of the 1950s.

NATIONAL BASEBALL HALL OF FAME

Mayor Ivan Allen, Jr., at the topping ceremony for Atlanta Stadium.

World Series championship season of 1957.

As it turned out, the Braves were a team on the verge of greatness when they arrived in Milwaukee. Lefthander Warren Spahn already was one of the best pitchers in baseball. Third baseman Eddie Mathews, only a 21-year-old sophomore in 1953, led the league with 47 home runs. Hank Aaron would reach the scene in 1954.

Few ballparks have ever been home simultaneously for three such extraordinary players with so many productive years in front of them. And the supporting cast wasn't bad either.

In 13 seasons at County Stadium, the Braves never had a worse record than the 84-78 they posted in 1963. Besides winning two pennants, they finished second five times, including 1959 when they

lost a playoff for the pennant to the Dodgers.

But once-rabid Milwaukeeans soon were staying home in droves. In 1961, attendance barely reached 1.1 million. By mid-1963, there was a report that the franchise was looking to leave Milwaukee for Atlanta. Following the 1964 season, the Braves' board voted to move to Atlanta, but a court injunction forced the team to remain in Milwaukee one more year to fulfill its lease.

ATLANTA-FULTON COUNTY STADIUM

The story of Atlanta Stadium began when Ivan Allen, Jr., whose family was in the office supply business, decided in 1961 to run for mayor. Then 50 years old, Allen was president of the Atlanta Chamber of Commerce. He said in his campaign that if elected, he would build a modern sports stadium. At the time, major league sports had yet to invade the South, but the hope was that such a stadium would induce a team to try this fertile region.

When Allen was elected, he set out to fulfill his campaign promise. On April 15, 1964, ground was broken, and just 51 weeks later, the Braves and Detroit Tigers played an exhibition game to dedicate Atlanta Stadium. But not until October 21 did it become official that the Braves would be the stadium's tenant. Then in November, due to the threat of legal proceedings by Milwaukee County, the National League instructed the Braves to fulfill their lease by playing the 1965 season at County Stadium.

As it turned out, the new stadium was used by the minor league Crackers in 1965.

Atlanta Stadium was typical in design of other circular concrete and steel ballparks being constructed in places such as Cincinnati, St. Louis, Philadelphia and San Francisco during the same period. What was different was how quickly the Atlanta ballpark was completed. No other such facility had ever gone up in less than a year.

When the stadium opened, the home run distances were 325 feet down the lines, 375 feet to the power alleys and 402 feet to center field. When the Braves departed after Game 5 of the 1996 World Series, it was 330 to the foul poles and 385 in the power alleys, but the center-field fence remained 402 feet from home plate. Seating capacity at the three-tiered stadium changed slightly over the years, but it was listed at 52,710 in its final season.

The Braves' first regular season game at Atlanta Stadium was played April 12, 1966 against Pittsburgh. A sellout crowd announced at 50,671 saw the Braves and Pirates battle through 12 innings tied at 1-1. In the 13th, future Hall of Famer Willie Stargell hit a two-run homer off Atlanta starter Tony Cloninger, giving the visitors a 3-1 edge. Joe Torre hit his second solo home run of the game in the bottom of the 13th but the Braves lost, 3-2.

On April 8, 1974, Hank Aaron became the all-time home run king, breaking Babe Ruth's career record. No. 715 came in the fourth inning of the home opener off the Dodgers' Al Downing.

In 1991, the atmosphere at Atlanta-Fulton County Stadium changed considerably. A new era in Braves baseball was launched, and the old ballpark was transformed from a baseball morgue into the liveliest stadium in America when the Braves went from having the worst record in baseball in 1990 to the World Series.

In the last regular-season game at the stadium, the Braves beat the Montreal Expos, 3-1, on September 23, 1996. The final game, however, was Game 5 of the '96 World Series in which the Yankees' Andy Pettitte outdueled Atlanta's John Smoltz, 1-0.

THE FRONT DOOR

Early on the morning of August 2, the end came for Atlanta-Fulton County Stadium in less than 30 seconds. And just as suddenly, Turner Field had center stage all to itself.

With the push of a button, 1,600 pounds of explosives brought the circular, steel-and-concrete stadium crashing to the ground in a cloud of dust. It was one of the final steps in the transformation of

ATLANTA-FULTON COUNTY STADIUM LASTS*

(l-r) Phil Niekro, Hank Aaron and Dale Murphy were among former Braves who participated in a special farewell to the old stadium.

DATE: Sept. 23, 1996.

SCORE: Braves 3 - Montreal 1.

BATTER: Moises Alou, Montreal.

HIT: David Segui, Montreal.

BRAVES HIT: Ryan Klesko.

STOLEN BASE: Luis Polonia, Atlanta.

WINNING PITCHER: Greg Maddux.

ATTENDANCE: 49,083.

TIME OF GAME: 2:22.

BRAVES HOME RUN: Marquis Grissom on September 22.

POST-SEASON GAME: 1996 World Series Game 5, October 24; Yankees 1 - Braves 0.

*Regular season

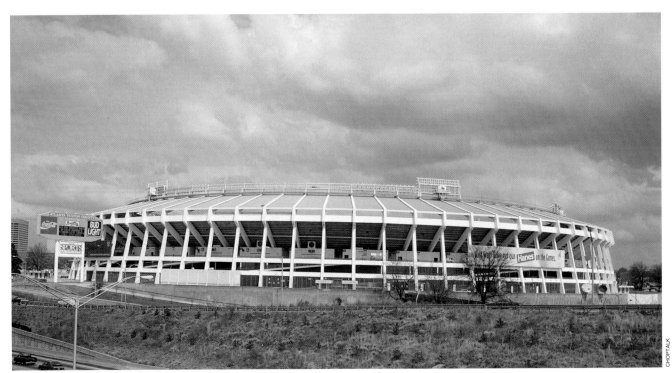

Opened in 1965, this familiar circular stadium was the Braves' home for 31 seasons from 1966-96.

the ballpark area that also included moving the Olympic cauldron and the construction of a parking lot on the site of the old stadium.

The implosion of 32-year-old Atlanta-Fulton County Stadium began on the north side and proceeded in both directions simultaneously, the structure collapsing in somewhat of a double-domino effect.

In the weeks leading up to the blast, the stadium's seats were sold and the building was gutted. Immediately after the implosion, work began on removing the tangled steel and crushing the concrete for use in the 4,000-plus-space parking lot.

Though the old stadium is gone, it will never be forgotten by Braves fans. In fact, the parking lot has been constructed in such a way that it serves as a monument to the facility that was built specifically to lure the Braves from Milwaukee and hence opened the South to major league sports.

Half of the retaining wall that surrounded the old stadium remains to accommodate a two-tiered, environmentally friendly design for the parking lot that was inspired by Ted Turner's wife, Jane Fonda, and

conceived by Henry Teague, chief architect for both Turner Field and Atlanta-Fulton County Stadium.

"The only time Jane Fonda got involved in this entire project was when she expressed concern about how much surface parking there was going to be, because it's bad from an environmental standpoint," said Janet Marie Smith, vice-president of sports and entertainment facilities for Turner Properties. "She personally asked for more environmentally conscious parking. Henry Teague worked with ECOS (Environmental Design), and he came up with the idea for keeping the old retaining wall. It was a win/win situation, because it was good from an environmental standpoint and it saved us $1.3 million."

The savings came from the fact that the two-tiered design meant there was no need to fill the 20-foot "hole" left where the old stadium sat.

"To the Braves' credit, they were willing to give up several hundred parking spaces and the revenue to do it this way," said Teague. "And I think it gave interest to something (a parking lot) that usually is mundane. It'll be a much better front door to Turner Field."

On the surface of the lot is a "ghosting" of the old playing field, with different colored "pavers" used to outline the infield, outfield, foul lines, warning track, etc. There is a monument in left field memorializing Hank Aaron's record-setting 715th home run. Special lighting sets off the site of the former playing field as a "special place," and rows of flags are placed on the retaining wall at the same angle as the steel canopy of the old stadium to create a profile of the former home of the Braves.

Additionally, the retaining wall will be decorated with artwork depicting a time line of memorable events at Atlanta-Fulton County Stadium. The project is expected to be completed in time for the opening of the Braves' 1998 season.

The "gateway" to Turner Field and the parking lot is provided by the Olympic cauldron, which was relocated from in front of Turner Field to a point north of the old stadium at the corner of Hank Aaron Drive and Fulton Street. The cauldron was re-dedicated on July 19, 1997, the one-year anniversary of the opening of the Centennial Olympic Games in Atlanta.

The Olympic cauldron was relocated from its original site between the stadiums to the corner of Hank Aaron Drive and Fulton Street.

In less than 30 seconds, Atlanta-Fulton County Stadium was reduced to a pile of rubble.

'Top: *The final touches were applied with care.* Bottom: (l) *Special "First Game" programs were hot items on Opening Night.* (r) *The Braves entertained over 3.4 million fans in Turner Field's Inaugural Season and had 33 sellouts.*

JUST THE FACTS

CHOPTALK

SEATING CAPACITY - 50,005
(includes 1,000 disabled/
companion seats)
Dugout level - 5,492 (includes 176
disabled/companion)
Terrace - 8,532 (391)
Field - 5,227 (159)
Club - 5,546 (66)
Field pavilion - 5,042 (247)
Terrace pavilion - 3,358 (62)
Upper level - 11,344 (38)
Upper pavilion - 4,098 (9)
Skyline - 190 (4)
Suite seats - 1,176
Standing room only - 3,000

SUITES

59 plus 3 party suites
accommodating 40-44 people
each
Size of seats - Width ranges from
19" to 22"
Distance between rows - 32"

Restrooms - 57 (women 28, men 29)
Stalls - 365 (women 291, men 74)
Distance from home plate to
backstop - 53'
Distance from 1st and 3rd bases to
dugouts - 45'
Parking spaces - 8,700 (after demo-
ition of Atlanta-Fulton County
Stadium)

BRAVESVISION

Overall structure size - 147' x 80'
Video screen - 29' x 38'
Fluorescent tube lights in video
board - 331,776
Video board weight - 21 tons
Matrix board - 32' x 64'
Scoreboard tomahawks - 15' high
with 44' span
Frequency of chops - every 2.2
seconds (for a complete chop)

MAX ANTON BIRNKAMMER

FIELD

Playing surface - 20' below street
level
Left field line - 335'
Left field power alley - 380'
Right field line - 330'
Right field power alley - 390'
Center field - 400'
Outfield fence - 8' high

THE PLAZA

Plaza video board - 22' x 16' 6"
Plaza matrix board - 72' x 3'
Number of TV monitors - 12
Picture of Hank Aaron's 715th
home run ball - 100 feet high
Seats in Chop House restaurant -
386
Seats in 755 Club - 905 indoors
and outdoors

MONUMENTS

6 retired numbers
3 statues / 1 bust

**SCOUTING REPORTS IN SCOUT'S
ALLEY** - 10 on walls; 200 in
interactive kiosk

MUSEUM ARTIFACTS - 200-plus

OTHER NUMBERS

Square footage - 1.3 million
Bricks - 1.265 million

— TURNER FIELD FIRSTS —
(APRIL 4, 1997 VS. CUBS UNLESS NOTED)

PITCH
Thrown by Denny Neagle, it was bunted by Brian McRae to Fred McGriff, who stepped on first base for the out.

ASSIST/PUTOUT
Fred McGriff on Brian McRae's first-inning bunt.

BRAVES BATTER
Kenny Lofton flied out to centerfielder Brian McRae.

HIT
Chipper Jones lined a single to left off Kevin Foster with two outs in the first.

EXTRA-BASE HIT/DOUBLE
Javy Lopez doubled to right-center leading off the second.

ALLISON SHIRREFFS

STRIKEOUT
Mark Lemke by Kevin Foster in the second.

STRIKEOUT BY A BRAVES PITCHER
Kevin Foster by Denny Neagle with two outs in the third.

HOME RUN
Michael Tucker to right field off Kevin Foster with one out and no one on base in the third.

GRAND SLAM
On April 14 in the seventh game at Turner Field, Javy Lopez homered to left off Cincinnati's Stan Belinda in the seventh inning, scoring Chipper Jones, Fred McGriff and Andruw Jones ahead of him.

TWO-HOMER GAME
On June 28, with the Braves decked out in replica 1938 Atlanta Black Crackers uniforms, Michael Tucker ruled — hitting a solo home run in the first and a three-run shot in the third, both off NL All-Star Curt Schilling — to pace a 9-1 whipping of the Phillies. To make things even sweeter, Tucker put on his show in front of a contingent of family and friends from his tiny hometown of Chase City, Virginia, and some 100 former Negro leaguers.

PINCH-HIT GRAND SLAM
With the Braves trailing the Phillies, 5-1, on June 29, Keith Lockhart came off the bench in the sixth inning to tie the game with a bases-loaded home run, leading to a 6-5 win.

RBI
Michael Tucker on his home run in the third.

RUN SCORED
Michael Tucker on his home run in the third.

TRIPLE/OPPONENT HIT
Brian McRae to lead off the fourth.

WALK
Chipper Jones with one out in the third by Kevin Foster.

PINCH-HIT/PINCH-HIT RBI
Keith Lockhart batted for Denny Neagle in the sixth and singled to right, driving in Ryan Klesko.

ERROR
Fred McGriff threw wildly to the plate in the seventh, allowing Jose Hernandez to score.

STOLEN BASE
Chipper Jones stole second in the seventh.

CAUGHT STEALING
Sammy Sosa was thrown out by Javy Lopez trying to steal second in the eighth.

GAME-WINNING HIT
Chipper Jones singled to left with two outs in the eighth, scoring Mike Mordecai.

DOUBLEPLAY
In the ninth, pinch-hitter Dave Hansen lined to Mark Lemke, who threw to first to double off Brant Brown, ending the game.

WINNING PITCHER
Brad Clontz.

LOSING PITCHER
Terry Adams.

SAVE
Mark Wohlers.

SHUTOUT/COMPLETE GAME
Greg Maddux and Mark Wohlers combined to beat the Cubs, 4-0, on April 6, but John Smoltz pitched the first complete-game shutout April 16, holding Cincinnati to six hits in a 3-0 victory.

Elevators - 11

Escalators - 5

Permanent concession stands - 67 with 700 employees; 9 operated by Aramark and 58 by non-profit groups that receive a portion of the proceeds

Portable concession stands - 50

Also: 100 vendors and 100 employees who work in two in-seat kitchens

Press box seats - 100-plus

Gallons of water the drainage system can accommodate - 102,000 per hour

Sand under turf - 7,500 tons.

Turf in playing area - 130,000 square feet

Lockers in Braves clubhouse - 44

Trash cans - 500-plus

Length of "Turner Field" sign over Braves administrative offices - 2,400 linear feet

Weight of "Turner Field" sign - 3,000 pounds

GAME DAY PERSONNEL

Ushers - 220

Guest relations staff - 110

Ticket takers - 75

Security officers - 125

Police - 50

MAX ANTON BIRNKAMMER

J. STOLL

Parking attendants - 65

ANNUAL CONCESSIONS

Hot dogs - 886,000

Soda - 297,750 gallons

Barbecue - 217,000 pounds

Cracker Jacks - 44,500 boxes

Peanuts - 365,000 bags

Popcorn - 96,000 bags

GROUND RULES

DUGOUTS

Dugouts are bounded by guard rails, and any ball hitting guard rails or netting is IN PLAY.

Ball hitting netting on home plate side of either dugout is IN PLAY.

Ball hitting facing over either dugout is dead - ONE BASE on pitch and TWO BASES on throw by a fielder. Catch may be made in either dugout.

BACKSTOP

Ball lodging in padding is dead - ONE BASE on pitch and TWO BASES on throw by a fielder.

CANVAS ON TARP DRUM

Catch may be made on canvas. Ball lodged behind or under canvas is dead - ONE BASE on pitch and TWO BASES on throw by a fielder.

FOUL POLES

Ball hitting any part of screen area supported by poles down left or right field line - HOME RUN.

OUTFIELD FENCE

Batted fly ball going over yellow line on top of outfield fence — HOME RUN.

— THE FIRST GAME —

CHICAGO CUBS VS. ATLANTA BRAVES
TURNER FIELD, APRIL 4, 1997

Game time weather: Cloudy - 71°.

CUBS' STARTING LINEUP
Brian McRae, CF
Doug Glanville, LF
Ryne Sandberg, 2B
Sammy Sosa, RF
Shawon Dunston, SS
Kevin Orie, 3B
Brant Brown, 1B
Scott Servais, C
Kevin Foster, P

BRAVES' STARTING LINEUP
Kenny Lofton, CF
Michael Tucker, RF
Chipper Jones, 3B
Fred McGriff, 1B
Ryan Klesko, LF
Javier Lopez, C
Mark Lemke, 2B
Jeff Blauser, SS
Denny Neagle, P

CUBS' FIRST
First pitch by Neagle at 7:47 p.m. McRae grounded out to McGriff, unassisted. Glanville flied out to Lofton. Sandberg flied out to Lofton. (O Runs, O Hits, O Errors, O LOB)

BRAVES' FIRST
Game delayed due to light failure at 7:52 p.m. Game re-started at 7:58 p.m. Lofton flied out to McRae. Tucker flied out to Glanville. C. Jones singled to left. McGriff singled up the middle; C. Jones advanced to second. Klesko flied out to Glanville. (O Runs, 1 Hit, O Errors, 2 LOB)

CUBS' SECOND
Sosa grounded out, Neagle to Blauser to McGriff. Dunston flied out to Klesko. Orie grounded out, Blauser to McGriff. (O Runs, O Hits, O Errors, O LOB)

BRAVES' SECOND
Lopez doubled to right-center. Lemke struck out swinging. Blauser flied out to Sosa; Lopez advanced to third. Neagle

struck out swinging. (O Runs, 1 Hit, O Errors, 1 LOB)

CUBS' THIRD
Brown grounded out, McGriff to Neagle. Servais popped out to Lemke. Foster struck out swinging. (O Runs, O Hits, O Errors, O LOB)

BRAVES' THIRD
Lofton flied out to McRae. Tucker homered to right on the first pitch. C. Jones walked. McGriff struck out swinging. Klesko flied out to Dunston. (I Run, 1 Hit, O Errors, 1 LOB) Braves 1, Cubs 0.

CUBS' FOURTH
McRae tripled to right-center. Glanville grounded out, Neagle to McGriff. Sandberg grounded out, Lemke to McGriff; McRae scored. Sosa popped out to McGriff. (1 Run, 1 Hit, O Errors, O LOB) Braves 1, Cubs 1.

BRAVES' FOURTH
Lopez popped out to Sandberg. Lemke singled to center. Blauser grounded out, Dunston to Brown; Lemke advanced to second. Neagle struck out swinging. (O Runs, 1 Hit, O Errors, 1 LOB)

CUBS' FIFTH
Dunston grounded out, Blauser to McGriff. Orie grounded out, McGriff unassisted. Brown singled to left. Servais flied out to Lofton. (O Runs, 1 Hit, O Errors, 1 LOB)

BRAVES' FIFTH
Lofton struck out swinging. Tucker singled to first. C. Jones grounded out, Sandberg to Brown; Tucker advanced to second. McGriff grounded out, Dunston to Brown. (O Runs, 1 Hit, O Errors, 1 LOB)

CUBS' SIXTH
Foster filed out to Lofton. McRae singled up the middle. Glanville singled to left, but was thrown out trying stretch it into a double, Klesko to C. Jones to Lemke; McRae advanced to

third. Sandberg doubled to left; McRae scored. Sosa was walked intentionally. Dunston grounded out, Lopez unassisted. (1 Run, 3 Hits, O Errors, 2 LOB) Cubs 2, Braves 1.

BRAVES' SIXTH
Klesko singled up the middle. Lopez singled through the hole at short; Klesko advanced to second. Lemke was retired on a sacrifice bunt, Foster to Sandberg; Klesko advanced to third and Lopez advanced to second. Blauser flied out to Dunston. Lockhart pinch-hit for Neagle and singled to right; Klesko scored, Lopez advanced to third but was thrown out trying to score, Sosa to Servais. (1 Run, 3 Hits, O Errors, 1 LOB). Braves 2, Cubs 2.

Ryan Klesko

CUBS' SEVENTH
Terrell Wade came in to pitch for the Braves, batting ninth. Orie struck out swinging. Brown grounded out, McGriff unassisted. Servais walked. Jose Hernandez pinch-hit for Foster and singled to center; Servais advanced to second. McRae singled to right; Servais scored; Hernandez reached third, then scored on McGriff's wild throw and McRae took second. Brad Clontz relieved Wade. Glanville grounded out, Blauser to McGriff (2 Runs, 2 Hits, 1 Error, 1 LOB.) Cubs 4, Braves 2.

BRAVES' SEVENTH
Patterson came in to pitch for the Cubs, batting ninth. Lofton singled to left. Tucker singled to right; Lofton advanced to third. C. Jones singled to right; Lofton scored, Tucker advanced

to third. McGriff struck out looking. C. Jones stole second. A. Jones pinch-hit for Klesko. Terry Adams relieved Patterson. A. Jones struck out swinging. Lopez filed out to Sosa. (1 Run, 3 Hits, 0 Errors, 2 LOB.) Cubs 4, Braves 3.

CUBS' EIGHTH

A. Jones went to right field, Tucker moved to left field. Sandberg walked. Sosa reached on a fielder's choice, Sandberg was forced out, C. Jones to Lemke. With Dunston batting, Sosa was caught stealing second, Lopez to Blauser. Dunston grounded out, C. Jones to McGriff. (0 Runs, 0 Hits, 0 Errors, 0 LOB).

BRAVES' EIGHTH

Lemke grounded out, Sandberg to Brown. Blauser singled to right. Mike Mordecai pinch-hit for Clontz and singled to left; Blauser advanced to second. Lofton reached first on Dunston's misplay of his grounder; Blauser scored and Mordecai advanced to second. Tucker filed out to Sosa. C. Jones singled to left; Mordecai scored and Lofton advance to third, but C. Jones was out trying to take second, Glanville to Dunston to Sandberg to Brown to Sandberg to Brown. (2 Runs, 3 Hits, 1 Error, 1 LOB). Braves 5, Cubs 4.

CUBS' NINTH

Wohlers came in to pitch for the Braves, batting ninth. Tyler Houston pinch-hit for Orie and struck out swinging. Brown walked. Dave Hansen pinch-hit for Servais and lined to Lemke, who threw to McGriff, doubling off Brown. (0 Runs, 0 Hits, 0 Errors, 0 LOB)

Mark Wohlers

BRAVES 5, CUBS 4
TURNER FIELD, ATLANTA
APRIL 4, 1997

CHICAGO CUBS	AB	R	H	RBI	ATLANTA BRAVES	AB	R	H	RBI
McRae, cf	4	2	3	1	Lofton, cf	5	1	1	0
Glanville, lf	4	0	1	0	Tucker, rf-lf	5	1	3	1
Sandberg, 2b	3	0	1	2	C. Jones, 3b	4	0	3	2
Sosa, rf	3	0	0	0	McGriff, 1b	4	0	1	0
Dunston, ss	4	0	0	0	Klesko, lf	3	1	1	0
Orie, 3b	3	0	0	0	c-A. Jones, ph-rf	1	0	0	0
e-Houston, ph	1	0	0	0	Lopez, c	4	0	2	0
Brown, 1b	3	0	1	0	Lemke, 2b	3	0	1	0
Servais, c	2	1	0	0	Blauser, ss	4	1	1	0
f-Hansen, ph	1	0	0	0	Neagle, p	2	0	0	0
Foster, p	2	0	0	0	a-Lockhart, ph	1	0	1	1
b-Hernandez, ph	1	1	1	0	Wade, p	0	0	0	0
Patterson, p	0	0	0	0	Clontz, p	0	0	0	0
Adams, p	0	0	0	0	d-Mordecai, ph	1	1	1	0
TOTALS	**31**	**4**	**7**	**3**	Wohlers, p	0	0	0	0
					TOTALS	**37**	**5**	**15**	**4**

a-Singled for Neagle in the 6th. b-Singled for Foster in the 7th. c-Struck out for Klesko in the 7th. d-Singled for Clontz in the 8th. e-Struck out for Orie in the 9th. f-Lined into a double play for Servais in the 9th.

CHICAGO CUBS	000	101	200	— 4
ATLANTA BRAVES	001	001	12X	— 5

E—Dunston; McGriff. DP—Atlanta 1 (Lemke and McGriff). LOB—Chicago 4, Atlanta 10. HR—Tucker (1) off Foster in the 3rd, 0 on. SB—C. Jones (1). CS—Sosa. S—Lemke (off Foster).

CHICAGO Cubs	IP	H	R	ER	BB	SO
Foster	6	9	2	2	1	5
Patterson	1/3	3	1	1	0	1
Adams (L, 0-1)	1-2/3	3	2	0	0	1
TOTALS	**8**	**15**	**5**	**3**	**1**	**7**

ATLANTA Braves	IP	H	R	ER	BB	SO
Neagle	6	5	2	2	1	1
Wade	2/3	2	2	1	1	1
Clontz (W, 1-0)	1-1/3	0	0	0	1	0
Wohlers (S, 2)	1	0	0	0	1	1
TOTALS	**9**	**7**	**4**	**3**	**4**	**3**

IBB — off Neagle 1 (Sosa).
U — Reliford, DeMuth, Dreckman and Darling. T—2:54. A—45,044.

— FIRST INTERLEAGUE GAME —
IN BRAVES HISTORY

ORIOLES 4, BRAVES 3
TURNER FIELD, ATLANTA JUNE 13, 1997

BALTIMORE ORIOLES	AB	R	H	RBI	ATLANTA BRAVES	AB	R	H	RBI
Anderson, cf	4	1	1	1	Blauser, ss	4	0	1	0
Alomar, 2b	3	1	1	0	Tucker, rf	4	0	1	0
Reboulet, 2b	1	0	0	0	C. Jones, 3b	4	1	1	1
Palmeiro, 1b	4	1	2	1	McGriff, 1b	2	0	0	0
C. Ripken, 3b	4	0	1	1	A. Jones, cf	3	1	1	0
Surhoff, lf	3	0	1	1	Perez, c	4	1	1	2
Webster, c	0	0	0	0	Klesko, lf	4	0	0	0
Hammonds, rf	4	0	1	0	Lemke, 2b	4	0	1	0
Hoiles, c	3	0	0	0	Maddux, p	2	0	0	0
Myers, p	0	0	0	0	Lopez, ph	1	0	1	0
Bordick, ss	3	1	1	0	Belliard, pr	0	0	0	0
Key, p	2	0	0	0	Embree, p	0	0	0	0
Benitez, p	0	0	0	0	Clontz, p	0	0	0	0
Orosco, p	0	0	0	0	Mordecai, ph	1	0	0	0
Tarasco, rf	0	0	0	0	**TOTALS**	**33**	**3**	**7**	**3**
TOTALS	**31**	**4**	**8**	**4**					

Baltimore Orioles	000	004	000	— 4
Atlanta Braves	000	000	120	— 3

DP—Baltimore 1, Atlanta 2. **LOB**—Baltimore 3, Atlanta 7. 3B—A. Jones (1). **HR**—C. Jones (8), Perez (2). SB—Tucker 2 (9). S—Key. SF—Surhoff.

Baltimore Orioles	IP	H	R	ER	BB	SO
Key (W,11-1)	6-2/3	5	1	1	3	6
Benitez	1	2	2	2	0	1
Orosco	1/3	0	0	0	0	1
Myers (S, 21)	1	0	0	0	0	1
TOTALS	**9**	**7**	**3**	**3**	**3**	**9**

Atlanta Braves	IP	H	R	ER	BB	SO
Maddux (L,7-3)	7	7	4	4	0	4
Embree	1-1/3	1	0	0	0	0
Clontz	2/3	0	0	0	0	1
TOTALS	**9**	**8**	**4**	**4**	**0**	**5**

HBP — by Maddux (Hoiles).
U — Wendelstedt, Nauert, Marsh, Kellogg. T—2:30. A—48,334.

— THE PLAYERS —

ATLANTA STADIUM DESIGN TEAM

Heery International, Inc., Atlanta, GA
Ellerbe Becket, Inc., Kansas City, MO
Rosser International, Inc., Atlanta, GA
Williams-Russell and Johnson, Inc.,
   Atlanta, GA
Allain Robinson McDuffie, Atlanta, GA
Cini-Little International, Inc.,
   Fort Lauderdale, FL
Harrington Engineers, Inc., East Point, GA
George C. Baird, Jr., PE, Atlanta, GA
Jones Worley Design, Inc., Atlanta, GA
Law Engineering, Inc., Atlanta, GA
R&D Testing and Drilling, Inc., Atlanta, GA
Leslie Design Associates, Inc., Atlanta, GA
Wrightson, Johnson, Haddon & Williams,
   Inc., Dallas, TX

DESIGNERS, CONTRACTORS, SUBCONTRACTORS & VENDORS

A.J. Concrete, Mableton, GA
ANDCO Sign Company, Charlotte, NC
A-One Signs, Norcross, GA
APAC GA, Smyrna, GA
ARCON Inc., Lawrenceville, GA
Absolute Total Communications,
   Lawrenceville, GA
Aesthetically Correct Design, Inc.,
   Atlanta, GA
Allied Fence Co., Mableton, GA
Alpha Insulation, Marietta, GA
Peter Ambler Associates, Boston, MA
Anatek Inc., Atlanta, GA
Ancha Electronics, Norcross, GA
Aramark, Atlanta, GA
Archer Sign Company, Atlanta, GA
Architectural Concepts, Inc., Tucker, GA
Associated Engineering Consultants, Inc.,
   Roswell, GA
Associated Space Design, Atlanta, GA
Atlanta History Center, Atlanta, GA
Atlanta Steel Erectors, Smyrna, GA
Barton Malow Company, Atlanta, GA
Beers Construction Co., Atlanta, GA
Bell-Mann, Atlanta, GA
Bell South, Atlanta, GA
Benise-Dowling, Decatur, GA
Berkel & Co., Austell, GA
Bliss Products, Douglasville, GA
Brooks & Black Fine Art & Framing, Inc.,
   Atlanta, GA
Butler Communications, Atlanta, GA
C.D. Moody, Lithonia, GA
CDA South, Inc., Atlanta, GA
Camatic Seating Company, Australia
Capital Signs, Inc., Atlanta, GA
Castone, Opelika, AL
Center Brothers, Atlanta, GA
Central Parking Systems, Atlanta, GA

Chairmasters, Inc., New York, NY
Cives Steel Co., Thomasville, GA
Clemens Construction, Lawrenceville, GA
Construction Services Unlimited, Hiram, GA
Construction Clean-Up Spec., Fairburn, GA
Contract Hardware, Atlanta, GA
Copeland Hirthler, Atlanta, GA
Corn Upholstery, Atlanta, GA
Corporate Environments, Inc., Atlanta, GA
Crettol Mayer Design, New York, NY
Custom Surfaces, Atlanta, GA
DPS Industries Inc., Mableton, GA
D'Agostino Izzo Quirk Architects, Inc.,
   Somerville, MA
Daktronics, Brookings, SD
David Ashton & Company, Baltimore, MD
Davis-Moye Associates, Inc., Atlanta, GA
Dixie Fence, East Point, GA
Dixie Store Fixtures, Birmingham, AL
Dywidag System International, Tucker, GA
ECOS Environmental Design, Atlanta, GA
E.L. Thompson, Atlanta, GA
Eastman Kodak, Rochester, NY
Eroman Anthony Engineers, Inc.,
   Somerville, MA
Express Color, Inc., Atlanta, GA
Foley Design, Inc., Atlanta, GA
Forte Design, Baltimore, MD
Freeman, Hapeville, GA
Gale Fireproofing, Riviera Beach, FL
Gary Lee Super Associates, Atlanta, GA
Georgia Tent & Awning, Atlanta, GA
Gilbert-Curry, Conley, GA
Glass Systems, Lithonia, GA
Greater Southern Distributing, Atlanta, GA
H.J. Russell & Co., Atlanta, GA
Duane Hatfield, Atlanta, GA
Henry Sign Company, Inc., Atlanta, GA
IDEAS, Inc., Tucker, GA
Illuminations Contract Lighting, Inc.,
   Atlanta, GA
Imaging Technologies, Inc., Atlanta, GA
Inglett & Stubbs, Atlanta, GA
Interactive Light, Los Angeles, CA
Internet Atlanta, Atlanta, GA
Jugs, Inc., Woodstock, GA
Karavan Doors, Fayetteville, GA
Knoll, Atlanta, GA
L.S. Decker, Houston, TX
Lazer-Tron, Inc., Pleasonton, CA
Lerch, Bates & Associates, Inc.,
   Norcross, GA
Llamas Coatings, Smyrna, GA
MIR Corportation, Lilburn, GA
Marek, Marietta, GA
Mayfield Rigging, Atlanta, GA
McLean Behm Steel Erectors, Inc.
McNamara Salvia Engineers,
   Somerville, MA
Membrane Systems, Inc.
Metro Waterproofing, Scottdale, GA
Metromont Materials, Greenville, SC
Montgomery Kone, Marietta, GA

Mortensen Woodwork, Union City, GA
Motz Group, Cincinnati, OH
Murphy & Orr, Atlanta, GA
NOVUS, Inc., Atlanta, GA
North Georgia Contracting,
   Cartersville, GA
North Georgia Sound, Alpharetta, GA
Northstar Fire Protection, Atlanta, GA
O.I. Jollay/Atlanta Masonry,
   Avondale Estates, GA
PROMATS, Inc., Ft. Collins, GA
Panasonic, Inc., Atlanta, GA
Paul Heard Co., Atlanta, GA
Polote Corp., Stone Mountain, GA
Precision Concrete Construction,
   Alpharetta, GA
Price & Sons, Union City, GA
Pro-Bel Enterprises Ltd., Pickering, Ontario
Pyramid Masonry, Decatur, GA
R.A. Banks, Atlanta, GA
Raker Construction, Atlanta, GA
Rockwell Group, New York, NY
Rouse-Wyatt Associates, Cincinnati, OH
Jeffrey Rubin, New York, NY
SKB, Inc., Atlanta, GA
Schott Corporation, Yonkers, NY
Section 10 Inc., Norcross, GA
Sign Simple, Atlanta, GA
Sims Corporation, Montgomery, AL
Skytek, Snellville, GA
Southern Commercial Waterproofing,
   Tucker, GA
Southern Pan, Conley, GA
Standard Iron, Inc., Chattanooga, TN
Steam Operations Corp., Birmingham, AL
Superior Rigging, Atlanta, GA
Technical Industries, Fairburn, GA
Total Quality/Mechanical, Alpharetta, GA
Triangle Signs, Balto, MD
U.S. Architectural Sales & Contracting,
   Marietta, GA
Universal Steel, Lithonia, GA
Van Brook of Lexington, Lexington, KY
Venitian Blind Services, Smyrna, GA
Visual Impressions, Charlotte, NC
WCC, Inc., Kennesaw, GA
Wadsworth-White Inc., Norcross, GA
Webnet Media, Atlanta, GA
Wells Communications, Dacula, GA
Wenger Construction, Smyrna, GA
Lynda Wilbanks, Atlanta, GA
Wilkerson-Comanche, Marietta, GA
Yancy & Jamieson, Atlanta, GA
Youngblood Design Studio, Marietta, GA

1997 GAME-BY-GAME AT TURNER FIELD

Gm.	Date	Opp.	W-L	Score	W/L Pitcher	Atl. HRs	Rec.	Pos.	GB	Att.
1	4/4	Chi	W	5-4	Clontz(1-0)	Tucker(1)	2-2	3	-1	*45,044
2	4/5	Chi	W	11-5	Smoltz(1-1)	Lopez(1)	3-2	T2	-1	45,698
3	4/6	Chi	W	4-0	Maddux(1-1)	C.Jones(2)				
						Blauser(1)	4-2	2	-1	41,318
4	4/8	Hou	W	4-2	Glavine(2-0)	–	5-2	2	-1	31,064
5	4/9	Hou	W	4-3(12)	Embree(1-0)	–	6-2	2	-.5	33,986
6	4/10	Hou	L	3-5	Smoltz (1-2)	McGriff(2)	6-3	2	-1.5	33,637

(5 Wins, 1 Loss on Homestand)

Gm.	Date	Opp.	W-L	Score	W/L Pitcher	Atl. HRs	Rec.	Pos.	GB	Att.
7	4/14	Cin	W	15-5	Neagle(1-0)	Lopez(2)	9-3	1	–	31,427
8	4/15	Cin	W	3-0	Smoltz(2-2)	–	10-3	1	+1	31,962
9	4/16	Cin	W	7-1	Byrd(1-0)					
					Blauser(2)	Lofton(1)	11-3	1	+1	38,411

(3-0 Homestand; 8-1 Season at Home)

Gm.	Date	Opp.	W-L	Score	W/L Pitcher	Atl. HRs	Rec.	Pos.	GB	Att.
10	4/25	SD	W	5-4	Neagle(3-0)	Lopez(4)				
						Lemke(1)	15-5	1	+4	43,376
11	4/26	SD	W	3-2(10)	Wohlers(1-0)	A.Jones(2)	16-5	1	+4	45,473
12	4/27	SD	W	2-0(5)	Maddux(3-1)	–	17-5	1	+4	36,399
13	4/28	LA	W	14-0	Glavine(4-0)	Lopez(5)				
						Blauser(3)	18-5	1	+4	29,357
14	4/29	LA	L	2-6	Wade(0-1)	Lopez(6)	18-6	1	+3	35,442

(4-1 Homestand; 12-2 Season at Home)

Gm.	Date	Opp.	W-L	Score	W/L Pitcher	Atl. HRs	Rec.	Pos.	GB	Att.
15	5/2	Pit	L	2-3	Bielecki(1-1)	Lemke(2)	20-7	1	+5	37,577
16	5/3	Pit	L	0-3	Glavine (4-1)	–	20-8	1	+4	46,602
17	5/4	Pit	W	3-1	Wade(1-1)	–	21-8	1	+5	42,037

(1-2 Homestand; 13-4 Season at Home)

Gm.	Date	Opp.	W-L	Score	W/L Pitcher	Atl. HRs	Rec.	Pos.	GB	Att.
18	5/13	Fla	L	5-11	Wade(1-3)	McGriff(6)	26-12	1	+4	38,365
19	5/14	Fla	L	3-4	Bielecki(1-3)	–	26-13	1	+3	38,902
20	5/16	StL	W	1-0(13)	Borowski(1-0)	–	27-13	1	+3	46,626
21	5/17	StL	W	11-6	Smoltz(5-3)	Blauser(6)	28-13	1	+3	*48,366
22	5/18	StL	W	5-1	Glavine(5-2)	–	29-13	1	+3	35,046
23	5/19	StL	W	7-3	Neagle(7-0)	C.Jones(5)	30-13	1	+3.5	33,497
24	5/20	Mon	W	4-2	Wade(2-3)	–	31-13	1	+3.5	38,278
25	5/21	Mon	W	3-2	Maddux(5-1)	Lockhart(1)	32-13	1	+4.5	41,528

(6-2 Homestand; 19-6 Season at Home)

Gm.	Date	Opp.	W-L	Score	W/L Pitcher	Atl. HRs	Rec.	Pos.	GB	Att.
26	5/29	SF	L	2-4	Smoltz(6-4)	–	35-16	1	+4.5	38,844
27	5/30	SF	W	3-2	Wohlers(2-0)	Klesko(8)	36-16	1	+4.5	45,181
28	5/31	SF	L	4-6	Borowski(2-1)	Klesko(9)	36-17	1	+4.5	46,445
29	6/1	SF	W	4-3	Bielecki(2-3)	Klesko(10)				
						Blauser(7)	37-17	1	+5.5	46,501
30	6/2	SD	L	4-5	Maddux(6-2)	–	37-18	1	+4.5	33,659
31	6/3	SD	L	2-5	Wohlers(2-1)	–	37-19	1	+4.5	41,902

(2-4 Homestand; 21-10 Season at Home)

Gm.	Date	Opp.	W-L	Score	W/L Pitcher	Atl. HRs	Rec.	Pos.	GB	Att.
32	6/13	Bal	L	3-4	Maddux(7-3)	C. Jones(8)				
						Perez(2)	42-23	1	+3.5	*48,334
33	6/14	Bal	L	4-6(12)	Borowski(2-2)	Lopez(12)	42-24	1	+3	*47,344
34	6/15	Bal	L	3-5(10)	Wohlers(2-2)	Blauser(8)	42-25	1	+2.5	*48,088

(0-3 Homestand; 21-13 Season at Home)

Gm.	Date	Opp.	W-L	Score	W/L Pitcher	Atl. HRs	Rec.	Pos.	GB	Att.
35	6/26	Phi	W	5-4	Neagle(11-1)	Graffanino(2)	49-28	1	+3.5	*47,962
36	6/27	Phi	W	7-1	Maddux(10-3)	A.Jones(6)				
						Blauser(11)	50-28	1	+4.5	*48,234
37	6/28	Phi	W	9-1	Smoltz(7-7)	Lopez(13)				
						C.Jones(13)				
						Tucker(7,8)	51-28	1	+4.5	*48,557
38	6/29	Phi	W	6-5	Bielecki(3-3)	Lockhart(3)	52-28	1	+4.5	*47,902

(4-0 Homestand; 25-13 Season at Home)

Gm.	Date	Opp.	W-L	Score	W/L Pitcher	Atl. HRs	Rec.	Pos.	GB	Att.
39	7/10	NYM	L	7-10	Bielecki(3-5)	C.Jones(15)				
						Perez(4)	57-31	1	+5.5	*47,685
40	7/11	NYM	L	7-9	Glavine(9-5)	McGriff(11)	57-32	1	+5.5	*49,094
41	7/12	NYM	W	7-4	Maddux(12-3)	Klesko(15)				
						Tucker(9)	58-32	1	+6	*48,091

Gm.	Date	Opp.	W-L	Score	W/L Pitcher	Atl. HRs	Rec.	Pos.	GB	Att.
42	7/13	NYM	L	6-7(10)	Bielecki(3-6)	–	58-33	1	+5	42,111
43	7/14	Phi	W	10-6	Millwood (1-0)	Klesko(16)				
						Spehr(1)	59-33	1	+5	38,118
44	7/15	Phi	L	1-8	Smoltz(8-8)	–	59-34	1	+5	39,494
45	7/16	Col	W	2-1	Glavine(10-5)	–	60-34	1	+5	*48,400
46	7/17	Col	W	8-2	Maddux(13-3)	Klesko(17,18)				
						Perez(5)	61-34	1	+5	*48,204
47	7/18	LA	W	4-1	Neagle(13-2)	McGriff(12)				
						A.Jones(8)	62-34	1	+6	*48,721
48	7/19	LA	L	1-4	Millwood(1-1)	Graffanino(3)	62-35	1	+5	*49,758
49	7/20	LA	L	3-8	Smoltz(8-9)	–	62-36	1	+5	*48,414
50	7/21	LA	W	5-4(10)	Embree(2-1)	McGriff(13)	63-36	1	+6	*49,318
(6-6 Homestand; 31-19 Season at Home)										
51	7/28	Chi	W	6-0	Neagle(14-2)	McGriff(15)	67-39	1	+7	47,266
52	7/29	Chi	W	7-2	Millwood(2-2)	A.Jones(12)				
						C.Jones(17)	68-39	1	+7.5	44,131
53	7/30	Chi	W	6-5	Embree(3-1)	–	69-39	1	+7.5	43,090
(3-0 Homestand; 34-19 Season at Home)										
54	8/6	StL	W	4-3	Wohlers(3-4)	Bautista(3)	72-43	1	+4.5	*46,880
55	8/7	StL	W	3-0	Neagle(16-2)	–	73-43	1	+5.5	*46,687
56	8/8	Fla	L	4-6	Byrd(3-2)	Blauser(14)	73-44	1	+4.5	*49,335
57	8/9	Fla	W	4-3	Smoltz(11-9)	–	74-44	1	+5.5	*47,552
58	8/10	Fla	L	2-4(10)	Bielecki(3-7)	–	74-45	1	+4.5	*47,649
59	8/11	Fla	W	2-1	Wohlers(4-4)	–	75-45	1	+5.5	*47,870
60	8/12	Pit	L	2-5	Wohlers(4-5)	–	75-46	1	+4.5	42,435
61	8/13	Pit	L	1-2	Smoltz (11-10)	–	75-47	1	+3.5	40,793
(4-4 Homestand; 38-23 Season at Home)										
62	8/22	Cin	W	6-2	Maddux(17-3)	McGriff(17)	79-49	1	+5	*48,937
63	8/23	Cin	W	10-3	Neagle(17-3)	Lofton(4)				
						A.Jones(14)	80-49	1	+5	*48,499
64	8/24	Cin	L	4-6(10)	Fox(0-1)	Lofton(5)	80-50	1	+4	*45,577
65	8/26	Hou	W	7-6(11)	Clontz(5-1)	Graffanino(4)				
						Lopez(20)	81-50	1	+4.5	37,313
66	8/27	Hou	L	4-6(13)	Byrd(3-3)	Graffanino(5)	81-51	1	+3.5	33,019
67	8/28	Hou	W	4-2	Neagle(18-3)	Lopez(21)				
						Klesko(19)	82-51	1	+4.5	37,849
(4-2 Homestand; 42-25 Season at Home)										
68	9/1	Det	L	2-4	Maddox(17-4)	–	85-52	1	+3.5	38,950
69	9/2	Det	W	5-0	Neagle(19-3)	Neagle(1)				
						Lockhart(5)				
						Lopez(22)	86-52	1	+3.5	32,308
70	9/3	Det	L	4-12	Smoltz(13-11)	Colbrunn(2)	86-53	1	+2.5	36,556
(1-2 Homestand; 43-27 Season at Home)										
71	9/12	Col	L	1-3	Wohlers(5-6)	Klesko(23)	91-55	1	+6.5	*47,772
72	9/13	Col	L	6-10	Cather(0-4)	Graffanino(7)	91-56	1	+5.5	*49,097
73	9/14	Col	L	0-4	Smoltz(14-12)	–	91-57	1	+4.5	*46,245
74	9/15	SF	W	5-4	Ligtenberg(1-0)	McGriff(22)	92-57	1	+5.5	38,641
75	9/16	SF	W	6-4	Millwood(4-3)	Perez(6)	93-57	1	+5.5	37,661
76	9/17	NYM	W	10-2	Maddux(19-4)	Klesko(24)				
						Blauser(17)	94-57	1	+6	40,974
77	9/18	NYM	W	11-4	Byrd(4-3)	C.Jones(21)				
						Tucker(12)	95-57	1	+6	41,373
78	9/19	Mon	W	2-1	Smoltz(15-12)	–	96-57	1	+6	*47,156
79	9/20	Mon	W	3-1	Glavine(14-7)	Lopez(23)	97-57	1	+7	*48,147
80	9/21	Mon	L	1-7	Neagle(20-4)	–	97-58	1	+7	*47,179
81	9/22	Mon	W	3-2(11)	Cather(1-4)	–	98-58	1	+8	41,268
(7-4 Homestand; 50-31 Season at Home)										

KEY - Gm. (Home game number); Opp. (Opponent); W-L (Win or Loss); W/L Pitcher (Braves pitcher of record); Atl. HRs (Braves home run hitters); Rec. (Team record); Pos. (Position in NL East standings); GB (Games behind division leader or margin of first-place lead; Att. (Attendance; * sellout).

— 1997 BRAVES STATISTICS AT TURNER FIELD —

BATTER	AVG	G	AB	R	H	2B	3B	HR	RBI	SH	SF	HP	BB	SO	SB	CS	GIDP	E
Simon	.444	9	9	1	4	0	0	0	1	0	0	0	0	0	0	0	1	0
Blauser	.325	74	255	48	83	12	4	9	32	0	1	8	37	48	3	1	7	6
Lofton	.322	63	258	49	83	7	3	3	23	0	1	2	32	40	14	11	4	2
C.Jones	.316	81	304	48	96	24	1	7	56	0	2	0	45	42	10	4	12	9
Colbrunn	.313	12	16	1	5	1	0	1	2	0	0	0	1	4	0	0	0	0
Lockhart	.309	48	55	10	17	2	1	3	14	1	1	0	7	8	0	0	0	1
Lopez	.306	59	183	24	56	9	0	11	34	1	3	3	23	41	0	1	4	1
Bautista	.293	33	41	9	12	1	2	1	3	1	1	1	2	9	1	0	1	1
Tucker	.280	69	239	34	67	10	4	5	22	3	1	2	21	55	9	3	5	4
Klesko	.270	72	230	28	62	10	3	10	44	0	2	2	26	58	1	2	8	3
McGriff	.265	78	294	39	78	14	1	8	52	0	5	2	33	60	2	0	12	10
Perez	.260	36	100	9	26	2	0	4	11	0	0	2	3	18	0	0	3	4
Lemke	.258	55	178	17	46	7	0	2	11	5	2	0	12	28	0	0	3	10
Graffanino	.253	57	99	13	25	4	0	5	11	3	3	0	13	22	2	4	1	2
A.Jones	.203	76	187	28	38	9	1	5	30	3	1	1	37	51	10	6	4	4
Spehr	.200	6	10	1	2	1	0	1	4	0	0	0	0	3	0	0	0	2
Pitchers	.173	81	162	14	28	2	0	1	14	18	0	0	12	54	2	1	0	9
Gregg	.143	6	7	0	1	1	0	0	0	0	0	0	0	0	0	0	0	0
Mordecai	.129	32	31	3	4	0	1	0	1	0	1	0	4	10	0	1	0	0
Belliard	.121	38	33	2	4	2	0	0	1	2	1	0	1	9	0	1	0	0
Giovanola	.000	9	6	0	0	0	0	0	0	0	0	0	1	1	0	0	2	0
Myers	.000	5	3	0	0	0	0	0	0	0	0	0	0	2	0	0	0	0
TOTALS	**.273**	**81**	**2,700**	**378**	**737**	**118**	**21**	**76**	**366**	**37**	**25**	**23**	**310**	**563**	**54**	**35**	**67**	**68**

(Key: AVG – batting average; G – games played; AB – at bats; R – runs scored; H – hits; 2B – doubles; 3B – triples; HR – home runs; RBI – runs batted in; SH – sacrifice hits; SF – sacrifices; HP – hit by pitch; BB – bases on balls; SO – strikeouts; SB – stolen bases; CS – caught stealing; GIDP – grounded into double play; E – errors)

PITCHER	ERA	W-L	G	GS	CG	SHO	SV	IP	H	R	ER	HR	HB	BB	SO	WP	OA
Fox	1.72	0-1	16	0	0	0	0	15.2	10	5	3	2	0	5	14	1	.169
Glavine	2.13	5-2	13	13	2	0	0	97.1	64	28	23	5	1	36	66	0	.186
Maddux	2.18	8-3	18	18	3	1	0	132.0	118	32	32	4	3	13	97	0	.244
Millwood	2.53	3-1	6	3	0	0	0	21.1	22	7	6	0	1	8	18	1	.265
Cather	2.63	1-1	22	0	0	0	0	24.0	13	7	7	0	2	12	21	0	.160
Ligtenberg	2.79	1-0	9	0	0	0	0	9.2	8	3	3	2	0	4	11	0	.216
Embree	2.96	3-0	37	0	0	0	0	27.1	22	9	9	1	2	13	29	2	.224
Neagle	3.06	10-1	18	18	2	2	0	120.2	102	48	41	14	2	22	85	2	.227
Smoltz	3.32	6-7	19	19	3	1	0	138.1	135	59	51	11	0	40	131	9	.254
Wade	3.82	2-2	8	6	0	0	0	30.2	42	16	13	3	1	11	27	1	.339
Clontz	4.01	2-0	25	0	0	0	0	24.2	24	11	11	2	0	9	21	0	.267
Bielecki	4.50	2-5	25	0	0	0	0	26.0	26	17	13	2	1	13	26	1	.248
Wohlers	4.76	4-4	37	0	0	0	15	34.0	30	20	18	3	0	18	42	3	.236
Borowski	5.59	1-2	8	0	0	0	0	9.2	9	7	6	1	0	9	4	0	.250
Byrd	7.16	2-2	18	2	0	0	0	27.2	27	24	22	4	3	19	17	2	.250
Brock	7.20	0-0	3	2	0	0	0	10.0	12	9	8	1	0	8	6	1	.316
TOTALS	**3.20**	**50-31**	**81**	**81**	**10**	**8**	**15**	**749.0**	**664**	**302**	**266**	**55**	**16**	**240**	**615**	**23**	**.238**

(Key: ERA – earned run average; W-L – won/loss record; G – games entered; GS – games started; CG – complete games; SHO – shutouts; SV – saves; IP – innings pitched; H – hits allowed; R – runs allowed; ER – earned runs allowed; HR – home runs allowed; HB – hit batsmen; BB – bases on balls allowed; SO – strikeouts; WP – wild pitches; OA – opponents' batting average)